wk1 11-70
wk2 127-163.
197-205

AMERICAN
SOCIAL
MOVEMENTS

THE CIVIL RIGHTS MOVEMENT

Nick Treanor, *Book Editor*

Daniel Leone, *President*
Bonnie Szumski, *Publisher*
Scott Barbour, *Managing Editor*
David M. Haugen, *Series Editor*

GREENHAVEN
PRESS®

THOMSON
GALE

San Diego • Detroit • New York • San Francisco • Cleveland
New Haven, Conn. • Waterville, Maine • London • Munich

LIBRARY OF CONGRESS CATALOGING-IN-PUBLICATION DATA

Civil rights / by Nick Treanor, book editor.
    p. cm. — (American social movements)
Includes bibliographical references and index.
ISBN 0-7377-1153-1 (pbk. : alk. paper) — ISBN 0-7377-1154-X (lib. : alk. paper)
    1. African Americans—Civil rights—History—20th century—Juvenile literature.
2. Civil rights movements—United States—History—20th century—Juvenile literature. 3. United States—Race relations—Juvenile literature. [1. African Americans—Civil rights—History—20th century. 2. Civil rights movements—History—20th century. 3. Race relations.] I. Treanor, Nick. II. Series.
E186.61 .C58 2003
323.1'196073'0904—dc21   2002001294

Printed in the United States of America

CONTENTS

Chapter 2 • SEGREGATION AND CIVIL DISOBEDIENCE

hypocrisy on the part of white liberals, though. Instead, it reflected new complexities in the civil rights movement.

Chapter 3 • RADICALIZATION AND A CHANGING MOVEMENT

broadened his focus from civil rights in the American South to the plight of the Vietnamese. The authors contemplate what would have happened, and what would the world be like now, if King had lived.

Chapter 4 • BROADENING THE AGENDA

What Remains to Be Done

by Nat Hentoff
The 1960s were basically an illusion. Whatever legal changes occurred, the essential position of black Americans remained unchanged. By the 1970s, blacks understood the need to assert and exercise control at the community level in order to improve their situation. Involving the younger generation of whites was a key factor in effecting real change.

The Origins of Affirmative Action
by Robert K. Fullinwider
Some people interpret affirmative action as giving preference to people of color in job selection or other types of social placement. Originally, however, it meant only conscious and deliberate effort to get rid of or minimize deep-seated discrimination. The shift in meaning occurred in the 1970s, when businesses started to talk of setting goals in hiring.

Chapter 5 • THE CLOSE OF THE CIVIL RIGHTS CENTURY

The Return of the Right

by James Oliver Horton and Lois E. Horton
Presidents Reagan and Bush were hostile toward the continuance and expansion of federal aid programs to minorities, and the last two decades of the twentieth century were characterized by a gradual shift toward the conservative right. Bill Clinton was more sympathetic, but his economic policies were not much different than those of his Republican predecessors.

Chapter 6 • Personal Narratives

tion. Although it has not been easy, civil rights protesters have overcome police dogs and water cannons to pursue their cause. King acknowledges that
the revolution will continue, whether or not he is
there to take part in all of its successes.

FOREWORD

Historians Gary T. Marx and Douglas McAdam define a social movement as "organized efforts to promote or resist change in society that rely, at least in part, on noninstitutionalized forms of political action." Examining American social movements broadens and vitalizes the study of history by allowing students to observe the efforts of ordinary individuals and groups to oppose the established values of their era, often in unconventional ways. The civil rights movement of the twentieth century, for example, began as an effort to challenge legalized racial segregation and garner social and political rights for African Americans. Several grassroots organizations—groups of ordinary citizens committed to social activism—came together to organize boycotts, sit-ins, voter registration drives, and demonstrations to counteract racial discrimination. Initially, the movement faced massive opposition from white citizens, who had long been accustomed to the social standards that required the separation of the races in almost all areas of life. But the movement's consistent use of an innovative form of protest—nonviolent direct action—eventually aroused the public conscience, which in turn paved the way for major legislative victories such as the Civil Rights Act of 1964 and the Voting Rights Act of 1965. Examining the civil rights movement reveals how ordinary people can use nonstandard political strategies to change society.

Investigating the style, tactics, personalities, and ideologies of American social movements also encourages students to learn about aspects of history and culture that may receive scant attention in textbooks. As scholar Eric Foner notes, American history "has been constructed not only in congressional debates and political treatises, but also on plantations and picket lines, in parlors and bedrooms. Frederick Douglass, Eugene V. Debs, and Margaret Sanger . . . are its architects as well as Thomas Jefferson and Abraham Lincoln." While not all

American social movements garner popular support or lead to epoch-changing legislation, they each offer their own unique insight into a young democracy's political dialogue.

Each book in Greenhaven's American Social Movements series allows readers to follow the general progression of a particular social movement—examining its historical roots and beginnings in earlier chapters and relatively recent and contemporary information (or even the movement's demise) in later chapters. With the incorporation of both primary and secondary sources, as well as writings by both supporters and critics of the movement, each anthology provides an engaging panoramic view of its subject. Selections include a variety of readings, such as book excerpts, newspaper articles, speeches, manifestos, literary essays, interviews, and personal narratives. The editors of each volume aim to include the voices of movement leaders and participants as well as the opinions of historians, social analysts, and individuals who have been affected by the movement. This comprehensive approach gives students the opportunity to view these movements both as participants have experienced them and as historians and critics have interpreted them.

Every volume in the American Social Movements series includes an introductory essay that presents a broad historical overview of the movement in question. The annotated table of contents and comprehensive index help readers quickly locate material of interest. Each selection is preceded by an introductory paragraph that summarizes the article's content and provides historical context when necessary. Several other research aids are also present, including brief excerpts of supplementary material, a chronology of major events pertaining to the movement, and an accessible bibliography.

The Greenhaven Press American Social Movements series offers readers an informative introduction to some of the most fascinating groups and ideas in American history. The contents of each anthology provide a valuable resource for general readers as well as for enthusiasts of American political science, history, and culture.

Black Americans and Civil Rights

M any students of American history think of the civil rights movement as a short and sharp period running from the landmark Supreme Court judgment in *Brown v. Board of Education* through the mid-1960s. It is certainly true that those years were intense ones that brought great change to the legal and social status of black Americans. It would be a mistake, however, to think that they exhaust the civil rights movement, which is better seen as a struggle that began far back in the days of slavery, perhaps even earlier than the republic itself. Those crucial years midcentury represent the high point of the movement—the culmination of many years of hard work—and so warrant the special attention this book affords them. However, it is important to understand the earlier civil rights struggles and the broader history of blacks in America.

SLAVES IN THE LAND OF THE FREE

By the time the Declaration of Independence announced on July 4, 1776, that "all men are created equal" and are endowed with the unalienable rights to "life, liberty and the pursuit of happiness," blacks had been enslaved on the continent for well over one hundred years. Nor did the declaration give enslaved blacks much reason to rejoice, as it would be nearly one hundred more years before the United States abolished slavery. Unlike white immigrants to America, almost all of whom came voluntarily, aspiring to find and make a new life for themselves, the vast majority of blacks who came to America's shores had been stolen from Africa and shipped to the new land against their will.

REACHING FOR FREEDOM

After the founding of the United States, Northern states gradually abolished slavery, yet it remained a strong institution in the South. There, slaves were used for harsh work, laboring on large plantations through the intense summers. Some slaves tried to escape to the North or to Canada, and what came to be known as the Underground Railroad developed, a secret system for transporting escaped slaves northward and for harboring them along the way. Soon a rift developed between the South, which fiercely clung to slavery, and the North, which increasingly frowned upon slavery in the South. The situation became more strained during the middle of the nineteenth century, when Northern abolitionists pressing the cause were bolstered by the success of such novels as Harriet Beecher Stowe's *Uncle Tom's Cabin*, which dramatized the plight of slaves. As well, the passage of the Fugitive Slave Act, which had been intended as part of a complex compromise between Northern and Southern states, served only to heighten tensions. The act authorized Southerners to pursue escaped slaves on Northern soil, and consequently had the result of bringing home to Northerners, many of whom had never before seen a captive slave, the horror of slavery.

EMANCIPATION

In 1861 President Abraham Lincoln announced in his inaugural address that he had "no purpose, directly or indirectly, to interfere with the institution of slavery in the states where it exists."[1] Yet calls for abolition mounted during the Civil War, particularly when the military value of emancipation as a means of crippling the South's resources became clear. Because the Confederacy had a slave labor force to work in its factories and produce its food, it could commit a greater percentage of its white men to the battlefield. Whatever Lincoln's motives may have been, he eventually decided to support abolishing slavery, and on January 1, 1863, he issued the Emancipation Proclamation, which freed all slaves in areas of rebellion. The Thirteenth Amendment, which was ratified in

December 1865, then prohibited slavery throughout the United States.

RECONSTRUCTION AND CIVIL RIGHTS

At the end of the Civil War, many questions remained about how the Confederate states would be accommodated in a renewed union. Furthermore, although all slaves had been freed, white southerners, who still controlled the southern states, were determined to keep blacks dependent and prevent them from gaining economic and political power. To this end they established the "black codes," a set of laws that ensured that blacks remained second-class citizens. All states guaranteed freed slaves certain basic rights, including the right to marry, enter into contracts, own property, and testify in court against other blacks. But the black codes, which varied from state to state, included some strong restrictions. There tended to be, for instance, a ban on interracial marriage, black jury service, and court testimony by blacks against whites. Furthermore, some states established racial segregation in public places, and in all southern states there were laws that limited economic opportunities for blacks, which were designed to keep blacks laboring on the plantations. For instance, in Mississippi blacks could not buy or sell farmland, and in South Carolina blacks wishing to enter nonagricultural employment needed a special license.

Some of the black codes were especially insidious and nurtured a relationship between white plantation owners and white law enforcement officials that was designed to control black labor. Blacks were officially free to sign labor contracts with plantation owners, for example, but those who failed to sign were often held to be vagrants and were auctioned off to employers who would pay the fines levied against them. In this way, many blacks found themselves living, once again, in virtual slavery despite the Emancipation Proclamation. Senator Lyman Trumbull of Illinois was outraged by the black codes and sought to have federal measures passed that would invalidate them. In March 1866 Congress passed a bill proposed by Trumbull that made black men American citizens with the

Flurry of Acts Amendments ...

same civil rights as all citizens; however, President Andrew Johnson vetoed the bill. Nonetheless, the Civil Rights Act of 1866 became the first major law ever passed over presidential veto when Congress overrode Johnson in April.

That same month Congress passed the Fourteenth Amendment, which declared that all persons (understood at the time to include only males) born or naturalized in the United States were citizens deserving equal protection of the law. As well, although this amendment did not guarantee black men the right to vote, it provided that any state that denied suffrage to black men would proportionally lose congressional representation. The Fifteenth Amendment, which was ratified in March 1870, made it illegal to deny suffrage to anyone because of race, color, or previous condition of servitude. Other notable pieces of Reconstruction legislation include the Enforcement Act of 1870, which provided for the protection of black voters; the Second Enforcement Act, which provided for federal supervision of elections in the South; and the Third Enforcement Act, which is also known as the Ku Klux Klan Act. That act was designed to target the Klan, which tried to prevent blacks from voting, and provided for stiffer penalties for such interference. Finally, the Civil Rights Act of 1875 made racial segregation illegal in transportation and public accommodations and forbade the barring of blacks from jury service.

THE LEGACY OF RECONSTRUCTION

The Reconstruction era, then, despite an initial attempt by southerners to keep blacks oppressed, was generally a great step forward for black civil rights. Progressive laws were matched by the gradual development of black institutions, such as Howard, Atlanta, and Fisk universities, all of which were founded between 1866 and 1868. Nonetheless, opportunities for black education remained severely limited. Furthermore, real economic opportunities for blacks remained rare, and an economic depression during the late 1870s led to widespread use of sharecropping, a farming system in which plantation lands were divided into small units and were rented out to farmers who paid the rent with a share of the crop. This system tended to trap sharecroppers, both black and white, in a system of debt peonage from which escape was difficult. Thus, although Reconstruction did bring meaningful legal changes, those changes were not well matched by meaningful social and economic changes. By and large black Americans, especially in the southern states, remained poor and powerless.

JIM CROW LAWS

Whereas Reconstruction was generally a step forward for the legal rights of black Americans, the concluding decades of the nineteenth century were surely a step backward. Those decades saw the rise of what came to be known as Jim Crow laws, the effect of which was to reduce the civil rights of blacks in the South. In some cases, legal advances won during Reconstruction were themselves nullified, as was the case in 1883 when the Supreme Court invalidated the Civil Rights Act of 1875, ruling that the Fourteenth Amendment only barred discrimination by the government, not by individuals. Gradually, an elaborate system of legal discrimination and segregation developed in the South. Blacks and whites were kept separate in buses, streetcars, trains, schools, parks, public buildings, and even cemeteries. Furthermore, those facilities open to blacks tended to be of much lower quality, and blacks everywhere in the United States generally lived in the dilapidated quarters of towns and cities and labored in menial, low-paying jobs. Their rights to vote were restricted in southern states through the use of poll taxes, property ownership or residency requirements, and literacy tests. Blacks were also expected to act deferentially toward whites in the South at all times, and they were often insulted or beaten when they failed to do so. Particularly vile was the practice, common in the South, of mobs lynching black men. White law enforcement officials, when not actively participating in these crimes, tended to look the other way; consequently black southerners migrated in huge numbers to the North, where they hoped to find better opportunities for themselves.

The Jim Crow system was sanctioned by the Supreme Court in its landmark 1896 decision in *Plessy v. Ferguson*. Homer Plessy was a black shoemaker in Louisiana who, with the support of a group of politically active blacks known as the Comite des Citoyens, decided to test the constitutional basis of the Jim Crow laws. In 1892 Plessy boarded a train in New Orleans bound for Covington, Louisiana, and sat down in the white section, where he was promptly arrested. John Ferguson, the local judge who ruled on the case, rejected Plessy's argument that the Separate Car Act violated the Fourteenth Amendment, which guarantees all citizens equal protection under the law. Ferguson declared that Louisiana had a right to regulate railroads within its borders in order to prevent racial mixing, and he held that the Fourteenth Amendment guaranteed blacks only legal equality, not social equality. Under appeal, the Louisiana Supreme Court upheld the decision, as did the U.S. Supreme Court in 1896, which ruled that states could maintain separate facilities for whites as long as blacks were not denied facilities of their own. The lone dissenting voice was that of Associate Justice John Marshall Harlan, who insisted that the Constitution was color blind. The Supreme Court ruling in *Plessy v. Ferguson* established the "separate but equal" doctrine, which gave legal sanction to segregation in the South for the next sixty years.

A VOICE FOR COMPROMISE

Although one might expect that blacks were universally opposed to the doctrine of separate but equal, this is not the case. Perhaps the most prominent black leader at the time was Booker T. Washington, and the year before the Supreme Court's historic judgment in *Plessy v. Ferguson*, Washington himself urged his own version of separate but equal. In a famous address to a white audience in Atlanta in 1895, Washington insisted that blacks had to concentrate on developing basic vocational skills, and he suggested that blacks and whites could live separately and yet work together. The policy he pushed was one of patience in the face of segregation and disenfranchisement, and this theme was welcomed by white Americans, who tended to be in no hurry to see a society in which black Americans were fully equal.

Black reaction to Washington's gradualism was more mixed. Certainly many blacks agreed with Washington, but there were numerous voices of dissent, particularly in the North. W.E.B. Du Bois, the first black American to earn a Ph.D. (from Harvard in 1895), was perhaps Washington's most prominent critic. In his 1903 book *The Souls of Black Folk*, Du Bois demanded full access to education for blacks, rejecting Washington's view that blacks should cultivate manual skills first. Du Bois was a striking figure; he was assertive and confident in an age when blacks were expected to be deferential. Furthermore, he clearly possessed a powerful and cultivated intellect, the depth and subtlety of which surprised and unsettled white racists.

EARLY CIVIL RIGHTS ORGANIZATIONS

In 1909 the Niagara Movement, a group of black activists headed by Du Bois, joined up with a group of progressive whites led by newspaper publisher Oswald Garrison Villard, the grandson of abolitionist William Lloyd Garrison, to found the National Association for the Advancement of Colored People. The association rejected Washington's approach and called for full political equality for blacks and an end to all racial discrimination. It also criticized the lynchings common in the South and the federal government for doing nothing about them. One of its chief projects involved providing legal assistance and representation to blacks in southern states, and it fought to overturn laws that restricted the voting rights of blacks. Within five years the organization had six thousand members and was rapidly gaining influence.

Another prominent organization during the first part of the century was the Brotherhood of Sleeping Car Porters, which, under the leadership of Asa Philip Randolph, organized black railroad workers to demand better wages and working conditions. A series of strikes, demonstrations, marches, and court battles won concessions for black workers, and Randolph successfully merged his group into the American Federation of Labor, which gave blacks new job opportunities and hooked their fortunes to those of the broader labor movement.

BLACK NATIONALISM AND THE HARLEM RENAISSANCE

In addition to these organized political activities, the growing concentration of blacks in the North, particularly in New York City, contributed to a flowering of black culture and arts during the 1920s known as the Harlem Renaissance. Music and theater, including all-black shows on Broadway, were an important part of the burst of creative activity, but most important of all was the rise of black literature. Gifted young writers, such as Langston Hughes, Nella Larsen, Claude McKay, and Jean Toomer, explored the black experience in novels, poems, and short stories, and they gained a national audience with the 1925 publication of *The New Negro*, an anthology of such writing. For the most part, though, black artists were forced to depend on white patronage, which could prove fickle. Langston Hughes's patron, for instance, a rich white member of Manhattan society, cut him off in anger after his poems moved from evoking the African soul to exploring the lives of working-class blacks in New York.

Although the Harlem Renaissance was not political activity in a narrow sense, it was intimately connected to rising nationalism within the black community. The most prominent black nationalist of the time was Marcus Garvey, a Jamaican who saw in the mass migrations of blacks from the South into the North an opportunity to reach a wider audience. In 1916 Garvey moved the headquarters of his Universal Negro Improvement Association from Jamaica to New York City, and within a few years he had set up branches in most major northern cities. Garvey was a gifted speaker, and his black audiences were held all the more captive by the fact that Garvey, unlike the society in which they lived, glorified blacks. Approximately eighty thousand blacks joined Garvey's association, which urged economic cooperation among blacks and a mass return to Africa, where Garvey hoped to found a black nation that would be powerful enough to defend the rights of blacks around the world. His movement collapsed, however, when he was jailed and then deported for fraud in connection to one of his business ventures. Nonetheless, Garvey's black nationalist movement foreshadowed a similar movement during the 1960s known as the black power movement.

WORLD WAR II

During the 1930s, with the entire United States in the grip of the Great Depression, black concerns had a hard time standing out as anything special. It was not until World War II that black leaders were again able to command a place on the stage. The National Association for the Advancement of Colored People saw the war against Nazi racism as an opportunity to embarrass the government, and membership in the organization swelled tenfold, reaching nearly five hundred thousand in 1945. At the same time, the Congress of Racial Equality, a new civil rights organization, started adopting the method of nonviolent resistance used successfully against British imperialists by the Indian spiritual leader Mohandas Gandhi. Its sit-ins helped eliminate segregated public facilities in Detroit, Denver, and Chicago, and they inspired other groups to adopt the technique. As well, Asa Philip Randolph, the leader of the Brotherhood of Sleeping Car Porters, called for one hundred thousand blacks to take part in a march on Washington, D.C. President Franklin D. Roosevelt, eager to avoid the march, agreed to Randolph's demands to end discrimination in government departments and in army, navy, air corps, and defense jobs.

The war also saw nearly 1 million black men and women serve in the armed forces, and combat needs slowly forced the end of policies limiting the role played by blacks in the military. Nonetheless, the great majority of units were segregated, and there were numerous racial conflicts which saw, by war's end, more than fifty blacks killed. Of particular irony is the fact that the Red Cross kept separate blood banks for white and black blood using a process for storing blood plasma that had been invented by a black doctor, Charles Drew. The tensions within the armed forces were matched by problems on American soil, as race riots broke out in numerous cities, including New York and Detroit. Furthermore, it was particularly poignant that these troubles occurred just as the United States was engaged against the terribly racist Nazis, and many people, in America and overseas, had no trouble seeing similarities between Hitler's reviled racism and the racism of much of white America.

POSTWAR PROGRESS

In 1947 the Committee on Civil Rights, which had been formed by President Harry Truman, released a report entitled *To Secure These Rights*. The report pointed to pervasive discrimination and called for more economic opportunities for blacks and stronger federal efforts to combat discrimination. Truman responded to the report by ordering the swift desegregation of the armed forces and by forming the Fair Employment Practices Commission, which was to ensure that blacks had a fair shot at getting federal jobs. As well, thousands of black soldiers returning from the war were given a chance to gain a college education through the GI Bill.

In 1950 the Legal Defense Fund, which had grown out of the National Association for the Advancement of Colored People, won two important cases that helped challenge the legal foundation of segregation. The group was successful in arguing that Herman Sweatt, who, as the only black student at the segregated University of Texas Law School, was in classrooms all by himself, was being denied the opportunity to receive equal training for a career in law. It also won in *McLaurin v. Oklahoma State Regents* when the Supreme Court ruled that John McLaurin, a black doctoral student who was forced to sit in a special "colored" section in his classrooms, was being denied an equal education. The real breakthrough came, however, in 1954 with the Supreme Court's ruling in *Brown v. Board of Education of Topeka, Kansas*, which concerned Linda Brown, a black student who was bused across town to attend a black school even though she lived closer to a white school. Civil rights lawyers argued that school segregation, which invariably left black schools badly underfunded, denied black students equal protection of the law. The Supreme Court agreed, unanimously ruling that the 1896 decision in *Plessy v. Ferguson* was contrary to the Fourteenth Amendment's guarantee of equal protection. Separating black schoolchildren, the court ruled, harmed them and was inherently unequal. The justices concluded that "in the field of public education, the doctrine of 'separate but equal' has no place. Separate education facilities are inherently unequal."[2] In a separate judgment, the Court ordered states to integrate their school systems "with all deliberate speed."[3]

THE SOUTHERN MANIFESTO

Although the legal ruling was in place to end school segregation, missing was a willingness to enforce the law of the land. The most northern of the southern states quietly integrated, and President Dwight Eisenhower directed officials in Washington, D.C., to desegregate classrooms in the capital. But Eisenhower refused to enforce the ruling in the Deep South, maintaining that the legal rulings could do little to change the minds of those committed to maintaining segregation. White legislators in the South made it clear that they had no intention of complying with the law, and in 1956 more than one hundred members of Congress signed the Southern Manifesto, which called the decision in *Brown* "a clear abuse of judicial power." Furthermore, the manifesto argued that the separate but equal principle

> restated time and time again, became a part of the life of the people of many of the States and confirmed their habits, customs, traditions, and way of life. It is founded on elemental humanity and commonsense, for parents should not be deprived by Government of the right to direct the lives and education of their own children.[4]

The document also declared that the Supreme Court's ruling

was bound to do more harm than good and offered a different interpretation of the state of race relations in the South:

> This unwarranted exercise of power by the Court, contrary to the Constitution, is creating chaos and confusion in the States principally affected. It is destroying the amicable relations between the white and Negro races that have been created through 90 years of patient effort by the good people of both races. It has planted hatred and suspicion where there has been heretofore friendship and understanding.[5]

The year closed with schools in the Deep South remaining 100 percent segregated.

The most blatant defiance of federal authority occurred in Little Rock, Arkansas, in 1957, when Governor Orval Faubus called on the state's National Guard to stop nine black students from entering Central High School despite a federal court order. Eisenhower stalled, but when the National Guard, having been withdrawn by Faubus under a new court order, was replaced by a jeering mob of nearly a thousand whites, Eisenhower acted. He took the Arkansas National Guard under his command and sent federal troops to protect the students. Faubus, determined to preserve segregation, closed down all of the high schools in Little Rock in 1958 and 1959. As the fifties ended, four years after the Supreme Court had ruled that desegregation was to proceed "with all deliberate speed" fewer than 1 percent of black students in the South attended desegregated schools.

Although the events in Little Rock captured national and international attention, similar stories were playing out at schools and universities throughout the South. As well, black activists, galvanized by the federal government's unwillingness to compel compliance with the Supreme Court's ruling, took the fight for desegregation beyond the schools. In Montgomery, Alabama, for instance, Rosa Parks was arrested on December 1, 1955, for refusing to give up her seat on a municipal bus to a white person. Local civil rights leaders quickly organized a boycott of city buses and established the Montgomery

Improvement Association, with Rev. Martin Luther King Jr. as its president, to coordinate the boycott. Blacks stayed off the buses until November 1956, when the Supreme Court ordered the city to desegregate the buses and the association called an end to the boycott. Similar boycotts were tried in other cities throughout the South, with varying success.

THE SPREAD OF PROTEST

In January 1957, building on the success of the Montgomery boycott, the Southern Christian Leadership Conference (SCLC) was founded to involve Christian churches in the civil rights struggle. King, the SCLC's first president, was attracted to the principles of nonviolent resistance, and he used the philosophy of nonviolence to great success, often in the face of considerable brutality by white policemen and mobs. Sit-ins quickly spread throughout the southern states, at segregated lunch counters and in hotels, theaters, libraries, parks, and other public places. Particularly noteworthy was a sit-in at the lunch counter of the Woolworth's department store in Greensboro, North Carolina, which lasted two months and involved dozens of students. Gradually, most of the signs reading "whites only" and "colored" came down.

Other noteworthy moments in the civil rights struggles of the late 1950s and early 1960s include the Freedom Rides; the movements in Albany, Georgia, and Birmingham, Alabama; the integration of the universities of Alabama and Mississippi; and the March on Washington. The Freedom Rides followed a 1960 Supreme Court decision that ended segregation in bus and railroad terminals and were designed to draw attention to continued attempts by white southerners to enforce segregation. The plan involved two buses of whites and blacks who were to travel from Washington, D.C., to New Orleans, attempting to integrate rest stops and restaurants along the way. The riders encountered hostility and police harassment wherever they stopped, and in Anniston, Alabama, a mob of angry whites forced one of the buses off the road, set it on fire, and attacked the passengers. The passengers of the other bus were no more fortunate. Although they made it to Birmingham, they were violently attacked by whites, and several of them were severely injured. The local police, although they knew about the attack, did nothing to stop it. In fact, later Freedom Riders who tried to continue the project were harassed by the police and were even arrested for disturbing the peace.

The pattern of police brutality continued in Albany, Georgia, where blacks in 1961 demonstrated for voting rights and an end to segregation. The local police arrested thousands of people, and when city jails filled, they shipped those they arrested to the jails of neighboring communities. They even arrested King, but when he vowed to stay in jail until demands were met, local officials, wary of his influence, agreed to make reforms and let him go. They later reneged on their deal, and the Albany movement ultimately accomplished little. More successful were the protests in Birmingham, Alabama, which again involved hundreds of arrests, including that of King. Eventually President John F. Kennedy intervened and pressured Birmingham officials to adopt reforms. Nonetheless, it was not long before local police used dogs and firehoses on blacks who had lined up to register to vote, and arrested three thousand demonstrators. The attacks were broadcast across the country and helped turn American public sympathy, and federal government resolve, toward efforts to secure civil rights.

FEDERAL SUPPORT, AT LAST

In September 1962 President Kennedy had placed the Mississippi National Guard under federal control after riots broke out at the University of Mississippi when James Meredith, who had a Supreme Court order assuring him admission to the university's law school, arrived on campus. In June 1963 Kennedy again had to face integration problems at a southern state university after Alabama's Governor George Wallace, whose inaugural speech had pledged "segregation today, segregation tomorrow, segregation forever!"[6] blocked two black students from entering the registration building of the University of Alabama. Wallace cast the issue as a clear one of unwarranted federal interference in an issue properly within the jurisdiction of the state, and he declared himself a defender of the Constitution. Kennedy forced Wallace to capitulate, however, and addressed the nation on television and radio, calling racism a clear moral wrong plaguing all of America. He also pressed white northerners, who tended to favor desegregation but counseled slow reform in the face of violent southern racism, to understand the black person's need for immediate change. "Who among us would be content to have the color of his skin changed and stand in his place?" Kennedy asked. "Who among us would then be content with the counsels of patience and delay?"[7] Tragically, the same night that Kennedy urged the nation to reject racism, a sniper in Jackson, Mississippi, killed Medgar Evers, the head of that state's branch of the National Association for the Advancement of Colored People.

Kennedy's words proved to be more than empty eloquence; within a week he had proposed comprehensive civil rights legislation that promised to ban discrimination in all public accommodations and strengthen voting rights. When Congress stalled on the bill, however, several civil rights groups organized a massive march on Washington in which an estimated 250,000 people took part. Gathered before the Lincoln Memorial, one hundred years after the Emancipation Proclamation, marchers spent a day listening to speeches and songs by black and white church leaders and social activists, the highlight of which perhaps was King's famous speech in which he declared his dream of an America free from racism. Although the march demonstrated the depth of popular support, it was not able to persuade Congress to pass Kennedy's civil rights bill. Nor did the bombing just three weeks later of the Sixteenth Street Baptist Church in Birmingham, Alabama, which killed four young black girls, speed up passage of the bill. It finally passed in July of the following year under Lyndon B. Johnson, who became president after Kennedy's assassination. 1964

Although one might think that passage of the Civil Rights Act would have boosted the spirits of civil rights activists, by the mid-1960s optimism was beginning to wane. The 1964 murders in Mississippi of three civil rights workers active in a voter registration drive—James Chaney, Andrew Goodman, and Michael Schwerner—were a hard blow to the movement. The mob that killed them included a local sheriff, but local officials refused to prosecute the case, and a local white supremacist judge, Harold Cox, dismissed federal charges of civil rights violations against the killers. That same summer, a group of blacks argued before the Democratic National Convention's rules committee that the Mississippi delegation was not legitimate because the state Democratic Party had unlawfully excluded blacks from registering and voting. Their effort to have the Mississippi delegation excluded was unsuccessful, however, and they themselves were thrown out of the convention. Furthermore, it soon became clear that the Civil Rights Act did not do enough to protect blacks from voter discrimination. Throughout the South, and especially in Alabama, blacks were prevented from voting with arrests and violence. A planned march from Selma to Montgomery, the state capital, which was meant to highlight the need for voting rights, ended just outside Selma when state troopers tear-gassed the peaceful marchers and beat them with clubs. A few days later, when marchers returned to try again, they were again forced to disperse, and one of the ministers, James Reeb, was beaten so severely by white supremacists that he died shortly thereafter. In response, President Johnson introduced a new voting rights bill in Congress, and he closed his speech by echoing the rallying cry of the civil rights movement, "We shall overcome." The Selma to Montgomery march eventually was completed under the protection of four thousand Alabama National Guardsmen, U.S. Army troops, and U.S. marshals.

A CHANGING MOVEMENT

Around 1965 the focus of the civil rights movement shifted from legally enforced segregation in the South to economic and social hardship in the North. But that was not the only change. The southern movement had been characterized by a commitment to nonviolence, whereas black leadership in the

North often did not hesitate to insist that blacks had a right to resist violence with violence. One such leader was Malcolm X, an assertive black nationalist with a commanding presence who was assassinated in 1965. He believed, much as Marcus Garvey had four decades earlier, that blacks had to learn to love themselves before they could worry about loving white people, and an important part of that, for him, included a commitment to act in their own defense when necessary. The movement in the North was also different in that it did not face obviously discriminatory laws and violently racist white leaders. Segregation in the North did not depend on legal support but on cold economic facts; whites and blacks tended to live in different parts of town and attend different schools and shop at different businesses because whites had money and blacks did not. Yet a further difference was that in the southern states, it was white supremacists who committed acts of violence, whereas in the northern cities it was more likely to be impoverished and frustrated blacks who turned to violence by rioting.

After 1965 many black activists, particularly in the North, became convinced that whites would never accept them as equals. Consequently, they turned away from advocating integration and instead opted for black power—the development of black institutions and racial pride. The call for black power resonated with many black people, especially in the urban North. In a 1966 newspaper article Stokely Carmichael, one of the chief proponents of black power, explained the notion as follows:

> Black power can be clearly defined for those who do not attach the fears of white America to their questions about it. We should begin with the basic fact that black Americans have two problems: they are poor and they are black. All other problems arise from this two-sided reality. . . . We had to begin with politics because black Americans are propertyless people in a country where property is valued above all. We had to work for power, because this country does not function by morality, love, and nonviolence, but by power.[8]

Although Stokely's understanding of power was largely political, other groups emphasized a different interpretation. Members of the Black Panther Party for Self-Defense, an important organization based in Oakland, California, carried firearms openly and called on blacks to retaliate against police brutality. The group enjoyed considerable support until it was eventually crushed by the FBI.

The shifting emphasis from southern de jure segregation to northern de facto segregation was accompanied by a sharp shift in white public opinion in the North, which had tended to support civil rights activism since the days of Reconstruction. Whites seemed to be tired of black concerns, and they showed less and less interest in black issues as the 1960s drew to a close. Furthermore, the drama of the Vietnam War and growing antiwar protest captured much of the national attention. With the assassination of King in 1968, the movement lost its most charismatic leader, and when presidential hopeful Robert Kennedy, who had strongly supported the black agenda, was assassinated shortly thereafter, it seemed to be the end of an era.

AFFIRMATIVE ACTION AND CLASS DIFFERENCES

As the 1970s opened, black Americans across the country generally enjoyed the same legal rights, at least officially, as white Americans did. The greatest remaining source of discontent was the economic and social disadvantages wrought by 250 years of slavery followed by 100 years of severe discrimination. Even if it was no longer legal to discriminate against blacks, it was thought to be hardly fair play to expect black people to compete successfully when most positions in society of any power and influence were held by whites. As President Johnson memorably put it in 1965, "You do not take a person who for years has been hobbled by chains and liberate him, bring him up to the starting line of a race, and say, 'you are free to compete with all the others,' and still justly believe that you have been completely fair."[9] Consequently, the late

1960s and 1970s saw the rise of affirmative action programs that were designed to make universities and businesses more accessible to blacks. Under these programs, black enrollment in colleges rose steadily, and new employment opportunities opened up, swelling the ranks of the black middle class. On the whole, blacks remained disadvantaged, but they did make modest economic gains throughout the 1970s. Furthermore, although the strong majority of television and movie actors remained white, it became less uncommon to see representations of black life and culture on screens across the country.

In a sense there came to exist two black worlds in America. One was populated by the black middle class, the clearest beneficiaries of the civil rights struggles, who held decent white-collar jobs and owned their own homes. *The Cosby Show*, a popular comedy during the 1980s starring Bill Cosby as a doctor married to a lawyer, portrayed this upwardly mobile black world. Yet no one could deny that there remained another black world in America, a place of inner-city poverty, where half the young people never finished high school and where the jobless rate during the late 1980s approached 60 percent. The much discussed economic plans of President Ronald Reagan, which cut taxes massively in order to stimulate the economy, brought little joy to these neighborhoods. As well, during the 1980s crack cocaine became common in urban ghettos; consequently, violent crime and gang activity rose, linked to the drug trade. In that decade, for instance, a young black male was six times more likely to be murdered than a young white male; in 1987 alone, the Bloods and the Crips, two major gangs in Los Angeles, were responsible for over four hundred killings. In addition, the pregnancy rate in urban ghettos soared, trapping huge numbers of young, poor, and uneducated women, and their children, in a vicious cycle of welfare dependency. For every black American who managed to make it into the middle class, there were others mired in urban ghettoes by complex social and economic forces beyond their control.

Although the issues that most concerned black leaders during the 1980s continued to vex them in the final decade of the twentieth century, new concerns arose as well. One was a lingering complaint over police brutality in urban centers, which was thrust into the public eye by the brutal beating of Rodney King by Los Angeles police officers and was kept there by police in New York City, who on several occasions gunned down unarmed black men or terrorized them in station houses. Increasing attention was also drawn to the judicial system itself, which seemed to many people to mete out justice more harshly to black defendants, and to the practice of racial profiling, which subjected blacks to greater police scrutiny. In addition, although the United States has only one-twentieth of the world's population, as the century drew to a close American prisons held one-quarter of the world's prisoners, and a disproportionate percentage of those prisoners were black. As obvious as it was that the civil rights movement, for all its successes, had not been able to ensure liberty, justice, and happiness for all, few politicians seemed willing to address the issue, and in the 2000 presidential election the problems of race were largely ignored. It may be that the civil rights movement is over, or it may be that its final chapter has not yet begun.

NOTES

1. Abraham Lincoln, First Inaugural Address, March 4, 1861, *Inaugural Addresses of the Presidents of the United States from George Washington 1789 to George Bush 1989.* Washington, DC: Government Printing Office, 1989, p. 134.

2. Earl Warren for the U.S. Supreme Court, *Brown v. Board of Education,* 347 U.S. 483 (1954). http://supreme.lp.findlaw.com/supreme_court/landmark3.html.

3. Earl Warren for the U.S. Supreme Court, *Brown v. Board of Education,* 349 U.S. 294 (1955). http://supreme.lp.findlaw.com/supreme_court/landmark3.html.

4. *Congressional Record,* 84th Cong., 2nd sess., 1956, 102, pt. 4: 4459–60.

5. *Ibid.*

6. George C. Wallace, Inaugural Address, 1963. www.archives.state.al.us/govs_list/inauguralspeech.html.

7. John F. Kennedy, Radio and Television Report to the American People on Civil Rights, June 11, 1963. www.jfklibrary.org/j061163.htm.

8. Stokely Carmichael, "What We Want," *New York Review of Books,* September 22, 1966, pp. 5–7.

9. Lyndon B. Johnson, "Commencement Address at Howard University: 'To Fulfill These Rights,' June 4, 1965." www.lbjlib.utexas.edu/johnson/archives.hom/speeches.hom/650604.asp.

CHAPTER 1

RECONSTRUCTION AND THE QUEST FOR EQUALITY

AMERICAN
SOCIAL
MOVEMENTS

What Should Be Done with the Freed Slaves?

FREDERICK DOUGLASS

Frederick Douglass was a very well known nineteenth century black abolitionist and former slave. In this piece, originally published by Douglass in his monthly newsletter in 1862, he addresses a question on the minds of many white people during the Civil War: What should be done with the slaves when they are freed? Douglass argues that nothing should be done with the freed slaves, that they should be left to their own resources and independence, just as white people are. He believes that, once free, former slaves should be treated exactly the same as white people and be given the same civil rights and the same economic opportunities. Douglass also argues forcefully against the proposal, common in some circles, to export former slaves back to Africa, from where they or their ancestors had been taken. Slaves are Americans, he argues, and should share in the fate of the nation.

W hat shall be done with the four million slaves if they are emancipated? This singular question comes from the same two very different and very opposite classes of the American people, who are endeavoring to put down the rebels [the Southern Confederates]. The first have no moral, religious, or political objection to Slavery, and, so far as they are concerned, Slavery might live and flourish to the end of time. They are the men who have an abiding affection for rebels, and at the beginning marched to the tune of "No Coercion—No subjugation." They have now dropped these unpopular "Noes"

Excerpted from "The Future of the Negro People of the Slave States," by Frederick Douglass, *Douglass' Monthly,* March 1862.

and have taken up another set, equally treacherous. Their tune now is, No Emancipation. No Confiscation of slave property, No Arming of the Negroes. They were driven from the first set of "Noes" by the gleaming of a half million bayonets, and I predict that they will be driven from the last set, though I cannot promise that they will not find another set.

The second class of persons are those who may be called young converts, newly awakened persons, who are convinced of the great evil and danger of Slavery, and would be glad to see some wise and unobjectionable plan of emancipation devised and adopted by the Government. They hate Slavery and love Freedom, but yet they are too much trammeled by the popular habit of thought respecting the Negro to trust the operation of their own principles. Like the man in the Scriptures, they see men only as trees walking. They differ from the first class only in motive and purpose, and not in premise and argument, and hence the answer to Pro-Slavery objections will answer those raised by our new anti-Slavery men. When some of the most potent, grave and reverend defenders of Slavery in England urged [abolitionist politician William] Wilberforce for a statement of his plan of Emancipation, his simple response was quit stealing.

My answer to the question, What shall be done with the four million slaves if emancipated? shall be alike short and simple: Do nothing with them, but leave them like you have left other men, to do with and for themselves. We would be entirely respectful to those who raise the inquiry, and yet it is hard not to say to them just what they would say to us, if we manifested a like concern for them, and that is; please to mind your business, and leave us to mind ours. If we cannot stand up, then let us fall down.—We ask nothing at the hands of the American people but simple justice, and an equal chance to live; and if we cannot live and flourish on such terms, our case should be referred to the Author of our existence. Injustice, oppression, and Slavery with their manifold concomitants have been tried with us during a period of more than two hundred years. Under the whole heavens you will find no parallel to the wrongs we have endured. We have worked without wages; we have lived without hope, wept without sympathy, and bled without mercy. Now, in the name of common humanity, and according to the laws of the Living God, we simply ask the right to bear the responsibility of our own existence.

INDEPENDENCE AND FAIR TREATMENT

Let us alone. Do nothing with us, for us, or by us as a particular class. What you have done with us thus far has only worked to our disadvantage. We now simply ask to be allowed to do for ourselves. I submit that there is nothing unreasonable or unnatural in all this request. The black man is said to be unfortunate. He is so. But I affirm that the broadest and bitterest of the black man's misfortunes is the fact that he is everywhere regarded and treated as an exception to the principles and maxims which apply to other men, and that nothing short of the extension of those principles to him can satisfy any honest advocate of his claims.

Even those who are sincerely desirous to serve us and to help us out of our difficulties, stand in doubt of us and fear that we could not stand the application of the rules which they freely apply to all other people.

Now, whence comes this doubt and fear? I will tell you. There is no difficulty whatever in giving ample and satisfactory explanation of the source of this estimate of the black man's capacity.

What have been his condition and circumstances for more than two centuries? These will explain all.

Take any race you please, French, English, Irish, or Scotch, subject them to slavery for ages—regard and treat them everywhere, every way, as property, as having no rights which other men are required to respect.—Let them be loaded with chains, scarred with the whip, branded with hot irons, sold in the market, kept in ignorance, by force of law and by common usage, and I venture to say that the same doubt would spring up concerning either of them, which now confronts the Negro. The common talk of the streets on this subject shows great ignorance. It assumes that no other race has ever been enslaved or could be held in slavery, and the fact that the black man submits to that condition is often cited as a proof of original and permanent inferiority, and of the fitness of the black man only for that condition. Just this is the argument of the Confederate States; the argument of Stephens in defense of S.C. [South Carolina]. But what are the facts? I believe it will not be denied that the Anglo-Saxons are a fine race of men, and have done something for the civilization of mankind, yet who does not know that this now grand and leading race was in bondage and abject slavery for ages upon their own native soil. They were not stolen away from their own country in small numbers, where they could make no resistance to their enslavers, but were enslaved in their own country.

Turn to the pages of the history of the Norman Conquest, by Monsieur Thierry, and you will find this statement fully attested.—He says: Foreigners visiting England, even so late as the sixteenth century, were astonished at the great number of serfs they beheld, and the excessive harshness of their servitude. The word bondage, in the Norman tongue, expressed at the time all that was most wretched in the condition of humanity. He again says: About the year 1381, all who were called bonds in English or in Anglo-Norman—that is, all the cultivators of land—were serfs in body and goods, obliged to pay heavy aids for the small portions of land which served them to feed their families, and were not at liberty to give up that portion of land without the consent of the Lords for whom they were obliged to do gratuitously their tillage, their gardening, and their carriage of all kinds. The Lords could sell them, together with their horses, their oxen, and their implements of husbandry—their children and their posterity—which in the English deeds was expressed in the following manner: Know that I have sold——, my knave, and all his offspring, born or to be born.

[English novelist] Sir Walter Scott, after describing very minutely the dress of a Saxon serf, says: One part of the dress only remains, but it is too remarkable to be suppressed. It was a brass ring resembling a dog's collar, but without any opening, and soldered fast around the neck, so loose as to form no impediment to breathing, and yet so tight as to be incapable of being removed excepting by the use of the file. On this singular gorget was engraved, in Saxon letters, an inscription of the following purport; Gurth, the son of Beowulph, is the born thrall of Cedric Rotherwood.

As an evidence of the contempt and degradation in which the Saxons were held, Monsieur Thierry says that after the conquest the Bishop of Lincoln reckoned only two languages in England—Latin for men of letters and French for the ignorant, in which language he himself wrote pious books for the use of the French, making no account of the English language and those who spoke it.

The poets of the same period, even those of English birth, composed all their verses in French when they wished to derive from them either profit or honor. Such is a brief view of the social condition occupied for ages by a people now the mightiest on the globe. The Saxon was of no account then; the Negro is of no account now. May not history one day carry the analogy a step further? In the case of the Saxon, we have a people held in abject slavery, upon their own native soil by strangers and foreigners. Their very language made no account of, and themselves wearing brass collars on their necks like dogs, bearing the names of their masters. They were bought and sold like the beast of the field, and their offspring born and to be born doomed to the same wretched condition. No doubt that the people of this now proud and grand race in their then abject condition were compelled to listen to disparagement and insults from their Norman oppressors, as galling as those which meet the black man here. No doubt that these disparagements hung about their necks like a mountain weight to keep them down, and no doubt there were men of shallow brain and selfish hearts to tell them that Slavery was their normal condition.

The misfortunes of my own race in this respect are not singular. They have happened to all nations, when under the heel of oppression. Whenever and wherever any particular variety of the human family has been enslaved by another, their slavers *true!* and oppressors, in every such instance, have found their best apology for their own base conduct in the bad character of their victims. The cunning, the deceit, the indolence, and the manifold vices and crimes, which naturally grow out of the condition of Slavery, are generally charged as inherent characteristics of the oppressed and enslaved race. The Jews, the Indians, the Saxons and the ancient Britons, have all had a taste of this bitter experience.

When the United States coveted a part of Mexico, and sought to wrest from that sister Republic her coveted domain, some of you remember how our press teemed from day to day with charges of Mexican inferiority—How they were assailed as a worn-out race; how they were denounced as a weak, worthless, indolent, and turbulent nation, given up to the sway of animal passions, totally incapable of self-government, and how excellent a thing we were told it would be for civilization ✓ if the strong beneficent arms of the Anglo-Saxon could be extended over them; and how, with our usual blending of piety with plunder, we justified our avarice by appeals to the handwriting of Divine Providence. All this, I say, you remember, for the facts are but little more than a dozen years old.

As between us and unfortunate Mexico, so it was with Russia and the Ottoman Empire. In the eyes of Nicholas, the Turk was the sick man of Europe—just as the Negro is now the sick man of America.

So, too, in former years, it was with England and Ireland. When any new burden was sought to be imposed upon that ill-fated country, or when any improvement in the condition of its people was suggested, and pressed by philanthropic and liberal statesmen, the occasion never failed to call forth the most angry and disparaging arguments and assaults upon the Irish race.

Necessity is said to be the plea of tyrants. The alleged inferiority of the oppressed is also the plea of tyrants. The effect upon these against whom it is directed is to smite them as with the hand of death. Under its paralyzing touch all manly aspirations and self-reliance die out and the smitten race comes almost to assent to the justice of their own degradation.

No wonder, therefore, that the colored people in America appear stupid, helpless and degraded. The wonder is rather that they evince so much spirit and manhood as they do. What have they not suffered and endured? They have been weighed, measured, marked and prized—in detail and in the aggregate. Their estimated value a little while ago was twenty hundred millions. Those twenty hundred millions of dollars have all the effect of twenty hundred millions of arguments against the Negro as a man and a brother. Here we have a mountain of gold, depending upon the continuance of our enslavement and degradation. No wonder that it has been able to bribe the press against us.—No wonder that it has been able to employ learning and eloquence against us. No wonder that it has bought up the American pulpit and obtained the sanction of religion against us. No wonder that it has turned every department of the Government into engines of oppression and tyranny toward us.—No nation, however gifted by nature, could hope to bear up under such oppressive weights.

Treat Freed Slaves Fairly

But to return. What shall be done with the four million slaves, if emancipated. I answer, deal justly with them; pay them honest wages for honest work; dispense with the biting lash, and pay them the ready cash; awaken a new class of motives in them; remove those old motives of shriveling fear of punishment which benumb and degrade the soul, and supplant them by the higher and better motives of hope, of self-respect, of honor, and of personal responsibility. Reverse the whole current of feeling in regard to them. They have been compelled hitherto to regard the white man as a cruel, selfish, and remorseless tyrant, thirsting for wealth, greedy of gain, and caring nothing as to the means by which he obtains it. Now, let him see that the white man has a nobler and better side to his character, and he will love, honor, esteem the white man. . . .

It is one of the strangest and most humiliating triumphs of

human selfishness and prejudice over human reason, that it leads men to look upon emancipation as an experiment, instead of being, as it is, the natural order of human relations. Slavery, and not Freedom, is the experiment; and to witness its horrible failure we have to open our eyes, not merely upon the blasted soil of Virginia and other Slave States, but upon a whole land brought to the verge of ruin.

We are asked if we would turn the slaves all loose. I answer, Yes. Why not? They are not wolves nor tigers, but men. They are endowed with reason—can decide upon questions of right and wrong, good and evil, benefits and injuries—and are therefore subjects of government precisely as other men are.

But would you have them stay here? Why should they not? What better is here than there? What class of people can show a better title to the land on which they live than the colored people of the South? They have watered the soil with their tears and enriched it with their blood, and tilled it with their hard hands during two centuries; they have leveled its forests, raked out the obstructions to the plow and hoe, reclaimed the swamps, and produced whatever has made it a goodly land to dwell in, and it would be a shame and a crime little inferior in enormity to Slavery itself if these natural owners of the Southern and Gulf States should be driven away from their country to make room for others—even if others could be obtained to fill their places. . . .

My friends, the destiny of the colored American, however this mighty war shall terminate, is the destiny of America. We shall never leave you. The allotments of Providence seem to make the black man of America the open book out of which the American people are to learn lessons of wisdom, power, and goodness—more sublime and glorious than any yet attained by the nations of the old or the new world. Over the bleeding back of the American bondman we shall learn mercy. In the very extreme difference of color and features of the Negro and the Anglo-Saxon, shall be learned the highest ideas of the sacredness of man and the fullness and perfection of human brotherhood.

No Time for Compromise or Submission

W.E.B. Du Bois

At the turn of the century, Booker T. Washington was the most visible black leader and was widely thought by white people to speak for blacks in America. Washington's strategy for black progress came to be known as the Atlanta Compromise after he outlined it in a speech to a mostly white audience in Atlanta in 1895. Washington's message stressed industry, patience, and tolerance, and, emphasizing the need for blacks to develop basic economic and commercial skills, downplayed the importance of civil and political rights. In this article, W.E.B. Du Bois, who was himself a well-known politically active black, criticizes this strategy. Du Bois is careful to recognize Washington's noble intentions but is harder on Washington's strategy, arguing that it fosters the idea that blacks are inferior to whites and requires them to settle for less than the full equality that Du Bois insists they deserve.

Easily the most striking thing in the history of the American Negro since 1876 is the ascendancy of Mr. Booker T. Washington. It began at the time when war memories and ideals were rapidly passing; a day of astonishing commercial development was dawning; a sense of doubt and hesitation overtook the freedmen's sons,—then it was that his leading began. Mr. Washington came, with a single definite programme, at the psychological moment when the nation was a little ashamed of having bestowed so much sentiment on Negroes, and was concentrating its energies on Dollars. His programme

Excerpted from *The Souls of Black Folk*, by W.E.B. Du Bois (Chicago, 1903).

of industrial education, conciliation of the South, and sub-mission and silence as to civil and political rights, was not wholly original; the Free Negroes from 1830 up to wartime had striven to build industrial schools, and the American Missionary Association had from the first taught various trades; and Price and others had sought a way of honorable alliance with the best of the Southerners. But Mr. Washington first indissolubly linked these things; he put enthusiasm, unlimited energy, and perfect faith into this programme, and changed it from a by-path into a veritable Way of Life. And the tale of the methods by which he did this is a fascinating study of human life.

It startled the nation to hear a Negro advocating such a programme after many decades of bitter complaint; it startled and won the applause of the South, it interested and won the admiration of the North; and after a confused murmur of protest, it silenced if it did not convert the Negroes themselves.

To gain the sympathy and cooperation of the various elements comprising the white South was Mr. Washington's first task; and this, at the time Tuskegee [a school founded by Washington to train black teachers] was founded, seemed, for a black man, well-nigh impossible. And yet ten years later it was done in the word spoken at Atlanta: "In all things purely social we can be as separate as the five fingers, and yet one as the hand in all things essential to mutual progress." This "Atlanta Compromise" is by all odds the most notable thing in Mr. Washington's career. The South interpreted it in different ways: the radicals received it as a complete surrender of the demand for civil and political equality; the conservatives, as a generously conceived working basis for mutual understanding. So both approved it, and to-day its author is certainly the most distinguished Southerner since [Confederate president] Jefferson Davis, and the one with the largest personal following.

BALANCING NORTH AND SOUTH

Next to this achievement comes Mr. Washington's work in gaining place and consideration in the North. Others less shrewd and tactful had formerly essayed to sit on these two stools and had fallen between them; but as Mr. Washington knew the heart of the South from birth and training, so by singular insight he intuitively grasped the spirit of the age which was dominating the North. And so thoroughly did he learn the speech and thought of triumphant commercialism, and the ideals of material prosperity, that the picture of a lone black boy poring over a French grammar amid the weeds and dirt of a neglected home soon seemed to him the acme of absurdities. One wonders what Socrates and St. Francis of Assisi would say to this.

And yet this very singleness of vision and thorough oneness with his age is a mark of the successful man. It is as though Nature must needs make men narrow in order to give them force. So Mr. Washington's cult has gained unquestioning followers, his work has wonderfully prospered, his friends are legion, and his enemies are confounded. To-day he stands as the one recognized spokesman of his ten million fellows, and one of the most notable figures in a nation of seventy millions. One hesitates, therefore, to criticise a life which, beginning with so little, has done so much. And yet the time is come when one may speak in all sincerity and utter courtesy of the mistakes and shortcomings of Mr. Washington's career, as well as of his triumphs, without being thought captious or envious, and without forgetting that it is easier to do ill than well in the world.

The criticism that has hitherto met Mr. Washington has not always been of this broad character. In the South especially has he had to walk warily to avoid the harshest judgments,—and naturally so, for he is dealing with the one subject of deepest sensitiveness to that section. Twice—once when at the Chicago celebration of the Spanish-American War he alluded to the color-prejudice that is "eating away the vitals of the South," and once when he dined with President Roosevelt— has the resulting Southern criticism been violent enough to threaten seriously his popularity. In the North the feeling has several times forced itself into words, that Mr. Washington's counsels of submission overlooked certain elements of true manhood, and that his educational programme was unnecessarily narrow. Usually, however, such criticism has not found open expression, although, too, the spiritual sons of the Abolitionists have not been prepared to acknowledge that the schools founded before Tuskegee, by men of broad ideals and self-sacrificing spirit, were wholly failures or worthy of ridicule. While, then, criticism has not failed to follow Mr. Washington, yet the prevailing public opinion of the land has been but too willing to deliver the solution of a wearisome problem into his hands, and say, "If that is all you and your race ask, take it."

OPPOSITION FROM BLACK AMERICANS

Among his own people, however, Mr. Washington has encountered the strongest and most lasting opposition, amounting at times to bitterness, and even to-day continuing strong and insistent even though largely silenced in outward expression by the public opinion of the nation. Some of this opposition is, of course, mere envy; the disappointment of displaced demagogues and the spite of narrow minds. But aside from this, there is among educated and thoughtful colored men in all parts of the land a feeling of deep regret, sorrow, and apprehension at the wide currency and ascendancy which some of Mr. Washington's theories have gained. These same men admire his sincerity of purpose, and are willing to forgive much to honest endeavor which is doing something worth the doing. They cooperate with Mr. Washington as far as they conscientiously can; and, indeed, it is no ordinary tribute to this man's tact and power that, steering as he must between so many diverse interests and opinions, he so largely retains the respect of all. . . .

But Booker T. Washington arose as essentially the leader not of one race but of two,—a compromiser between the South, the North, and the Negro. Naturally the Negroes resented, at first bitterly, signs of compromise which surrendered their civil and political rights, even though this was to be exchanged for larger chances of economic development. The rich and dominating North, however, was not only weary of the race problem, but was investing largely in Southern enterprises, and welcomed any method of peaceful cooperation. Thus, by national opinion, the Negroes began to recognize Mr. Washington's leadership; and the voice of criticism was hushed.

THE PROBLEM WITH WASHINGTON'S STANCE

Mr. Washington represents in Negro thought the old attitude of adjustment and submission; but adjustment at such a peculiar time as to make his programme unique. This is an age of unusual economic development, and Mr. Washington's programme naturally takes an economic cast, becoming a gospel of Work and Money to such an extent as apparently almost completely to overshadow the higher aims of life. Moreover, this is an age when the more advanced races are coming in closer contact with the less developed races, and the race-feeling is therefore intensified; and Mr. Washington's programme practically accepts the alleged inferiority of the Negro races. Again, in our own land, the reaction from the sentiment of war time has given impetus to race-prejudice against Negroes, and Mr. Washington withdraws many of the high demands of Negroes as men and American citizens. In other periods of intensified prejudice all the Negro's tendency to self-assertion has been called forth; at this period a policy of submission is advocated. In the history of nearly all other races and peoples the doctrine preached at such crises has been that manly self-respect is worth more than lands and houses, and that a people who voluntarily surrender such respect, or cease striving for it, are not worth civilizing.

In answer to this, it has been claimed that the Negro can survive only through submission. Mr. Washington distinctly asks that black people give up, at least for the present, three things,—

First, political power,
Second, insistence on civil rights,
Third, higher education of Negro youth,—

and concentrate all their energies on industrial education, the accumulation of wealth, and the conciliation of the South. This policy has been courageously and insistently advocated for over fifteen years, and has been triumphant for perhaps ten years. As a result of this tender of the palm-branch, what has been the return? In these years there have occurred:

Result.

1. The disfranchisement of the Negro
2. The legal creation of a distinct status of civil inferiority for the Negro
3. The steady withdrawal of aid from institutions for the higher training of the Negro

These movements are not, to be sure, direct results of Mr. Washington's teachings; but his propaganda has, without a shadow of doubt, helped their speedier accomplishment. The question then comes: Is it possible, and probable, that nine millions of men can make effective progress in economic lines if they are deprived of political rights, made a servile caste, and allowed only the most meager chance for developing their exceptional men?

THE PRESENT PARADOX

If history and reason give any distinct answer to these questions, it is an emphatic *No*. And Mr. Washington thus faces the triple paradox of his career:

"Triple Paradox"

1. He is striving nobly to make Negro artisans business men and property-owners; but it is utterly impossible, under modern competitive methods, for workingmen and property-owners to defend their rights and exist without the right of suffrage.
2. He insists on thrift and self-respect, but at the same time counsels a silent submission to civic inferiority such as is bound to sap the manhood of any race in the long run.
3. He advocates common-school and industrial training, and depreciates institutions of higher learning; but neither the Negro common schools, nor Tuskegee itself, could remain open a day were it not for teachers trained in Negro colleges, or trained by their graduates.

This triple paradox in Mr. Washington's position is the object of criticism by two classes of colored Americans. One class is spiritually descended from [leaders of slave rebellions] Toussaint the Savior, through Gabriel, Vesey, and Turner, and they represent the attitude of revolt and revenge; they hate the white South blindly and distrust the white race generally, and so far as they agree on definite action, think that the Negro's only hope lies in emigration beyond the borders of the United States. And yet, by the irony of fate, nothing has more effectually made this programme seem hopeless than the recent course of the United States toward weaker and darker peoples in the West Indies, Hawaii, and the Philippines,—for where in the world may we go and be safe from lying and brute force?

W.E.B. Du Bois

The other class of Negroes who cannot agree with Mr. Washington has hitherto said little aloud. They deprecate the sight of scattered counsels, of internal disagreement; and especially they dislike making their just criticism of a useful and earnest man an excuse for a general discharge of venom from small-minded opponents. Nevertheless, the questions involved are so fundamental and serious that it is difficult to see how men like the Grimkes, Kelly Miller, J.W.E. Bowen, and other representatives of this group, can much longer be silent. Such men feel in conscience bound to ask of this nation three things:

1. The right to vote
2. Civic equality
3. The education of youth according to ability

They acknowledge Mr. Washington's invaluable service in counselling patience and courtesy in such demands; they do not ask that ignorant black men vote when ignorant whites are debarred, or that any reasonable restrictions in the suffrage should not be applied; they know that the low social level of the mass of the race is responsible for much discrimination against it, but they also know, and the nation knows, that relentless color-prejudice is more often a cause than a result of the Negro's degradation; they seek the abatement of this relic of barbarism, and not its systematic encouragement and pampering by all agencies of social power from the Associated Press to the Church of Christ. They advocate, with Mr. Washington, a broad system of Negro common schools supplemented by thorough industrial training; but they are surprised that a man of Mr. Washington's insight cannot see that no such educational system ever has rested or can rest on any other basis than that of the well-equipped college and university, and they insist that there is a demand for a few such institutions throughout the South to train the best of the Negro youth as teachers, professional men, and leaders.

HIGHER IDEALS AND ASPIRATIONS

This group of men honor Mr. Washington for his attitude of conciliation toward the white South; they accept the "Atlanta Compromise" in its broadest interpretation; they recognize, with him, many signs of promise, many men of high purpose and fair judgment, in this section; they know that no easy task has been laid upon a region already tottering under heavy burdens. But, nevertheless, they insist that the way to truth and right lies in straightforward honesty, not in indiscriminate flattery; in praising those of the South who do well and criticising uncompromisingly those who do ill; in taking advantage of the opportunities at hand and urging their fellows to do the same, but at the same time in remembering that only a firm adherence to their higher ideals and aspirations will ever keep those ideals within the realm of possibility. They do not expect that the free right to vote, to enjoy civic rights, and to be educated, will come in a moment; they do not expect to see the bias and prejudices of years disappear at the blast of a trumpet; but they are absolutely certain that the way for a people to gain their reasonable rights is not by voluntarily throwing them away and insisting that they do not want them; that the way for a people to gain respect is not by continually belittling and ridiculing themselves; that, on the contrary, Negroes must insist continually, in season and out of season, that voting is necessary to modern manhood, that color discrimination is barbarism, and that

An Outcast at Home

On June 9, 1874, during congressional debate on the Civil Rights Bill of 1875, James T. Rapier, a black representative, rose to speak. In his address, he pointed to his own experience of discrimination to counter the argument that the bill was unnecessary because blacks already enjoyed equal civil rights.

I affirm, without the fear of contradiction, that any white ex-convict (I care not what may have been his crime, nor whether the hair on the shaven side of his head has had time to grow out or not) may start with me to-day to Montgomery, that all the way down he will be treated as a gentleman, while I will be treated as the convict. He will be allowed a berth in a sleeping-car with all its comforts, while I will be forced into a dirty, rough box with the drunkards, apple-sellers, railroad hands, and next to any dead that may be in transit, regardless of how far decomposition may have progressed. . . .

There is not an inn between Washington and Montgomery, a distance of more than a thousand miles, that will accommodate me to a bed or meal. Now, then, is there a man upon this floor who is so heartless, whose breast is so void of the better feelings, as to say that this brutal custom needs no regulation? I hold that it does and that Congress is the body to regulate it. . . .

black boys need education as well as white boys.

In failing thus to state plainly and unequivocally the legitimate demands of their people, even at the cost of opposing an honored leader, the thinking classes of American Negroes would shirk a heavy responsibility,—a responsibility to themselves, a responsibility to the struggling masses, a responsibility to the darker races of men whose future depends so largely on

Sir, in order that I might know something of the feelings of a freeman, a privilege denied me in the land of my birth, I left home last year and traveled six months in foreign lands, and the moment I put my foot upon the deck of a ship that unfurled a foreign flag from its mast-head, distinctions on account of my color ceased. I am not aware that my presence on board the steamer put her off her course. I believe we made the trip in the usual time. It was in other countries than my own that I was not a stranger, that I could approach a hotel without the fear that the door would be slammed in my face. Sir, I feel this humiliation very keenly; it dwarfs my manhood, and certainly it impairs my usefulness as a citizen. . . .

Mr. Speaker, to call this land the asylum of the oppressed is a misnomer, for upon all sides I am treated as a pariah. I hold that the solution of this whole matter is to enact such laws and prescribe such penalties for their violation as will prevent any person from discriminating against another in public places on account of color. No one asks, no one seeks the passage of a law that will interfere with any one's private affairs. But I do ask the enactment of a law to secure me in the enjoyment of public privileges.

James T. Rapier, speech on the Civil Rights Bill, June 9, 1874.

Three misconceptions & their solutions

this American experiment, but especially a responsibility to this nation,—this common Fatherland. It is wrong to encourage a man or a people in evil-doing; it is wrong to aid and abet a national crime simply because it is unpopular not to do so. The growing spirit of kindliness and reconciliation between the North and South after the frightful difference of a generation ago ought to be a source of deep congratulation to all, and especially to those whose mistreatment caused the war; but if that reconciliation is to be marked by the industrial slavery and civic death of those same black men, with permanent legislation into a position of inferiority, then those black men, if they are really men, are called upon by every consideration of patriotism and loyalty to oppose such a course by all civilized methods, even though such opposition involves disagreement with Mr. Booker T. Washington. We have no right to sit silently by while the inevitable seeds are sown for a harvest of disaster to our children, black and white. . . .

THREE MISCONCEPTIONS

It would be unjust to Mr. Washington not to acknowledge that in several instances he has opposed movements in the South which were unjust to the Negro; he sent memorials to the Louisiana and Alabama constitutional conventions, he has spoken against lynching, and in other ways has openly or silently set his influence against sinister schemes and unfortunate happenings. Notwithstanding this, it is equally true to assert that on the whole the distinct impression left by Mr. Washington's propaganda is, first, that the South is justified in its present attitude toward the Negro because of the Negro's degradation; secondly, that the prime cause of the Negro's failure to rise more quickly is his wrong education in the past; and, thirdly, that his future rise depends primarily on his own efforts. Each of these propositions is a dangerous half-truth. The supplementary truths must never be lost sight of: first, slavery and race-prejudice are potent if not sufficient causes of the Negro's position; second, industrial and common-school training were necessarily slow in planting because they had to await the black teachers trained by higher institutions,—it being extremely doubtful if any essentially different development was possible, and certainly a Tuskegee was unthinkable before 1880; and, third, while it is a great truth to say that the Negro must strive and strive mightily to help himself, it is equally true that unless his striving be not simply seconded, but rather aroused and encouraged, by the initiative of the richer and wiser environing group, he cannot hope for great success.

In his failure to realize and impress this last point, Mr. Washington is especially to be criticised. His doctrine has tended to make the whites, North and South, shift the burden of the Negro problem to the Negro's shoulders and stand aside as critical and rather pessimistic spectators; when in fact the burden belongs to the nation, and the hands of none of us are clean if we bend not our energies to righting these great wrongs.

The South ought to be led, by candid and honest criticism, to assert her better self and do her full duty to the race she has cruelly wronged and is still wronging. The North— her co-partner in guilt—cannot salve her conscience by plastering it with gold. We cannot settle this problem by diplomacy and suaveness, by "policy" alone. If worse comes to worst, can the moral fibre of this country survive the slow throttling and murder of nine millions of men?

The black men of America have a duty to perform, a duty stern and delicate,—a forward movement to oppose a part of the work of their greatest leader. So far as Mr. Washington preaches Thrift, Patience, and Industrial Training for the masses, we must hold up his hands and strive with him, rejoicing in his honors and glorying in the strength of this Joshua called of God and of man to lead the headless host. But so far as Mr. Washington apologizes for injustice, North or South, does not rightly value the privilege and duty of voting, belittles the emasculating effects of caste distinctions, and opposes the higher training and ambition of our brighter minds,—so far as he, the South, or the Nation, does this,—we must unceasingly and firmly oppose them.

A Program for Change

NATIONAL ASSOCIATION FOR THE
ADVANCEMENT OF COLORED PEOPLE

The National Association for the Advancement of Colored People was founded in 1910, and this document, written in 1919, outlines its project in those early years. The main goal of the organization was winning legal and political rights for black Americans rather than directly securing social and economic equality. The NAACP, as it is commonly known, believed that the Constitution guaranteed black Americans fair and equal treatment and challenged many laws on constitutional grounds. Although it enjoyed greatest influence in the 1950s and 1960s, the NAACP was founded early in the twentieth century and continues to be active today.

First and foremost among the objectives for 1919 must be the strengthening of the Association's organization and resources. Its general program must be adapted to specific ends. Its chief aims have many times been stated:

1. A vote for every Negro man and woman on the same terms as for white men and women.
2. An equal chance to acquire the kind of an education that will enable the Negro everywhere wisely to use this vote.
3. A fair trial in the courts for all crimes of which he is accused, by judges in whose election he has participated without discrimination because of race.
4. A right to sit upon the jury which passes judgment upon him.

Excerpted from "The Task for the Future—A Program for 1919," by the National Association for the Advancement of Colored People, *Report of the National Association for the Advancement of Colored People for the Years 1917 and 1918* (New York, 1919).

5. Defense against lynching and burning at the hands of mobs.
6. Equal service on railroad and other public carriers. This to mean sleeping car service, dining car service, Pullman service, at the same cost and upon the same terms as other passengers.
7. Equal right to the use of public parks, libraries and other community services for which he is taxed.
8. An equal chance for a livelihood in public and private employment.
9. The abolition of color-hyphenation and the substitution of "straight Americanism."

If it were not a painful fact that more than four-fifths of the colored people of the country are denied the above named elementary rights, it would seem an absurdity that an organization is necessary to demand for American citizens the exercise of such rights. One would think, if he were from Mars, or if he knew America only by reading the speeches of her leading statesmen, that all that would be needful would be to apply to the courts of the land and to the legislatures. Has not slavery been abolished? Are not all men equal before the law? Were not the Fourteenth and Fifteenth Amendments passed by the Congress of the United States and adopted by the states? Is not the Negro a man and a citizen?

When the fundamental rights of citizens are so wantonly denied and that denial justified and defended as it is by the lawmakers and dominant forces of so large a number of our states, it can be realized that the fight for the Negro's citizenship rights means a fundamental battle for real things, for life and liberty.

A FIGHT FOR WHITE AND BLACK

This fight is the Negro's fight. "Who would be free, himself must strike the blow." But, it is no less the white man's fight. The common citizenship rights of no group of people, to say nothing of nearly 12,000,000 of them, can be denied with impunity to the State and the social order which denies them.

This fact should be plain to the dullest mind among us, with the upheavals of Europe before our very eyes. Whoso loves America and cherishes her institutions, owes it to himself and his country to join hands with the members of the National Association for the Advancement of Colored People to "Americanize" America and make the kind of democracy we Americans believe in to be the kind of democracy we shall have in *fact*, as well as in theory.

The Association seeks to overthrow race prejudice but its objective may better be described as a fight against *caste*. Those who seek to separate the Negro from the rest of Americans are intent upon establishing a caste system in America and making of all black men an *inferior caste*. As America could not exist "half slave and half free" so it cannot exist with an upper caste of whites and a lower caste of Negroes. Let no one be deceived by those who would contend that they strive only to maintain "the purity of the white race" and that they wish to separate the races but to do no injustice to the black man. The appeal is to history which affords no example of any group or element of the population of any nation which was separated from the rest and at the same time treated with justice and consideration. Ask the Jew who was compelled to live in the proscribed Ghetto whether being held separate he was afforded the common rights of citizenship and the "equal protection of the laws?" To raise the question is to find the answer "leaping to the eyes," as the French say.

THE GOAL OF PUBLIC EQUALITY

Nor should any one be led astray by the tiresome talk about "social equality." Social equality is a private question which may well be left to individual decision. But, the prejudices of individuals cannot be accepted as the controlling policy of a state. The National Association for the Advancement of Colored People is concerned primarily with *public equality*. America is a nation—not a private club. The privileges no less than the duties of citizenship belong of right to no *separate class* of the people but to *all* the people, and to them as *individuals*. The constitution and the laws are for the protection of the minority and of the unpopular, no less than for the favorites of fortune, or they are of no meaning as American instruments of government.

Such a fight as has been outlined is worthy of the support of all Americans. The forces which seek to deny, and do deny, to the Negro his citizenship birthright, are powerful and intrenched. They hold the public offices. They administer the law. They say who may, and who may not vote, in large measure. They control and edit, in many sections, the influential organs of public opinion. They dominate. To dislodge them by legal and constitutional means as the N.A.A.C.P. proposes to endeavor to dislodge them, requires a strong organization and ample funds. These two things attained, victory is but a question of time, since justice will not forever be denied.

THE ORGANIZATIONAL PLAN

The lines along which the Association can best work are fairly clear. Its fight is of the brain and the soul and to the brain and the soul of America. *It seeks to reach the conscience of America.* America is a large and busy nation. It has many things to think of besides the Negro's welfare. In Congress and state legislatures and before the bar of public opinion, the Association must energetically and adequately defend the Negro's right to fair and equal treatment. To command the interest and hold the attention of the American people for *justice to the Negro* requires money to print and circulate literature which states the facts of the situation. And the appeal must be on the basis of the facts. It is easy to talk in general terms and abstractly. The presentation of concrete data necessitates ample funds.

Lynching must be stopped. Many Americans do not believe that such horrible things happen as do happen when Negroes are lynched and burned at the stake. Lynching can be stopped when we can reach the hearts and consciences of the American people. Again, money is needed.

Legal work must be done. Defenseless Negroes are every day denied the "equal protection of the laws" because there is not money enough in the Association's treasury to defend them, either as individuals or as a race.

Legislation must be watched. Good laws must be promoted wherever that be possible and bad laws opposed and defeated, wherever possible. Once more, money is essential.

The public must be kept informed. This means a regular press service under the supervision of a trained newspaper man who knows the difference between news and gossip, on the one hand, and mere opinion on the other. That colored people are contributing their fair share to the well-being of America must be made known. The war has made familiar the heroic deeds of the colored soldier. The colored civilian has been, and is now, contributing equally to America's welfare. If men have proven to be heroes in warfare, they must have had virtues in peace time. That law-abiding colored people are denied the commonest citizenship rights, must be brought home to all Americans who love fair play. Once again, money is needed.

The facts must be gathered and assembled. This requires effort. Facts are not gotten out of one's imagination. Their gathering and interpretation is skilled work. Research workers of a practical experience are needed. Field investigations, in which domain the Association has already made some notable contributions, are essential to good work. More money.

The country must be thoroughly organized. The Association's nearly 200 branches are a good beginning. A field staff is essential to the upbuilding of this important branch development. A very large percentage of the branch members are colored people. As a race they have less means, and less experience in public organization, than white people. But, they are developing rapidly habits of efficiency in organization. Money, again is needed.

But, not money alone is needed. Men and women are vital to success. Public opinion is the main force upon which the Association relies for a *victory of justice.*

$\mathcal{P}$

CHAPTER 2

SEGREGATION AND CIVIL DISOBEDIENCE

AMERICAN
SOCIAL
MOVEMENTS

Nonviolent Protest Achieves Desegregation and Voting Rights

1954-
1965

ALPHONSO PINKNEY

In this piece, Alphonso Pinkney, a retired professor at the City University of New York, looks at the ten years between the Supreme Court's *Brown v. Board of Education* ruling, which outlawed school segregation, and the Voting Rights Act of 1965. He notes that many whites were opposed to desegregation and that blacks had to resort to protests, sit-ins, and boycotts in their efforts to end segregation. He also outlines the violent response black protesters often faced and the resultant rise of white sympathy in the North. According to Pinkney, this crucial decade won greater civil rights for blacks, but did little to change the place of blacks as an oppressed underclass.

[handwritten margin notes: political not economic gains]

The post–World War II era has been a period of rapid change in the United States and in the world. Although changes affecting the status of black Americans have been neither rapid nor widespread, they have occurred and they have generated greater expectations. The resistance of white Americans to change has made blacks apprehensive about the willingness of society to accord them treatment equal to what its white citizens receive. The caution with which public officials have moved to make amends for what are rather widely regarded as past injustices has created greater black militancy. The depth of antiblack sentiment in society has frequently been indicated by the negative response of white Americans to in-

Excerpted from *Black Americans*, by Alphonso Pinkney (Upper Saddle River, NJ: Prentice-Hall, 1999). Copyright © 1999 by Prentice-Hall, Inc. Reprinted with permission.

creased black militancy. Because white Americans insist upon determining the pace with which changes in race relations occur, a crisis has resulted. Blacks have learned from experience that positive changes affecting their status are more likely to result from political pressures than from altruism. In the mid-1950s it appeared that increased civil rights for blacks might become one of the major tasks to which American society might address itself for the first time in a century.

BEGINNINGS OF THE REVOLT

The Supreme Court decision of May 1954 outlawing segregation in public education was welcomed by black Americans and their white supporters, who felt that somehow this act might signal the beginning of a new era in the relations between black and white Americans. The decision had been expected, and black Americans felt that it would afford white Americans, especially those in the South, the opportunity to share in the worldwide movement for greater human rights. White southerners responded to the desegregation ruling not with feelings of relief, but with the establishment, during the summer, of White Citizens' Councils, which had as their primary function massive resistance to the ruling of the Supreme Court. Since the Supreme Court did not indicate how its ruling was to be implemented, school districts that had either required or permitted segregation reopened in September on a segregated basis (except those in Washington, DC, and Baltimore, Maryland, where attempts were made to comply with the ruling of the Court). Throughout the South, plans were made to do whatever became necessary to maintain the long-standing practice of racial segregation in schools. Statements by public officials in that region (governors, senators, representatives) supported the notion of massive resistance.

When the Supreme Court finally issued its implementation decree—that desegregation in public education should proceed "with all deliberate speed"—in May 1955, the forces opposing integration in public education had already organized themselves throughout the South. Southerners were determined to maintain separate schools for black and white pupils, regardless of the ruling of the Supreme Court. The extent of their opposition came as a surprise to blacks and their white supporters. It appeared that their hopes for a new era in race relations would not materialize. If a ruling of the highest court in the country could be met with such contempt by those responsible for maintaining the constitutional rights of citizens, how could black people ever expect to be accorded rights equal to those of white Americans?

Signs of growing unrest were evident among black Americans. African colonies were demanding and receiving independence from European colonial powers, and it appeared that all of Africa would achieve political freedom before black people in the United States would be able to assert the fundamental rights of service in places of public accommodation or attendance at schools supported by taxes imposed on them. Later in the summer of 1955, Emmett Till, a 14-year-old black boy from Chicago, visiting in Money, Mississippi, was kidnapped and lynched. He was accused of having whistled at a white woman, and, characteristically, those responsible for his murder were never apprehended. Feelings of disillusionment were widespread in black communities.

THE MONTGOMERY BUS BOYCOTT

On December 1, 1955, a black seamstress, Rosa Parks, boarded a public bus in Montgomery, Alabama. She took a seat in the section set aside for blacks. Shortly thereafter she was ordered to vacate her seat so a white man could occupy it. She refused and was arrested. When word of the arrest spread through the black community, the Montgomery Bus Boycott was organized. The bus boycott lasted for more than a year, ending in December 1956, when the Supreme Court upheld a lower-court ruling outlawing racial segregation on buses in Montgomery.

This massive demonstration of solidarity among blacks in opposition to long-standing practices of segregation and discrimination can be considered the first major act of resistance by blacks in modern times and signaled the birth of what

Philosophy of non-violence

might be called the black revolt. The story of the Montgomery Bus Boycott spread throughout black communities in the United States and served as an impetus for similar acts in other cities. Tallahassee, Florida, and Birmingham, Alabama, followed with bus boycotts. Nonviolent resistance to what was considered an "evil" system composed of "unjust" laws became the official means of dealing with the caste system of the South. The philosophy of nonviolence, according to its principal spokesman, contains the following elements: (1) active resistance to "evil," (2) attempts to win over one's opponent through understanding, (3) directing one's attack against forces of "evil" rather than against persons performing such acts, (4) willingness to accept suffering, without retaliation, (5) refusal to hate one's opponent, and (6) the conviction that the universe is on the side of justice.

As the nonviolent resistance movement spread, massive opposition to social change in the realm of race relations was intensified by white southerners. One hundred southern members of Congress signed the Southern Manifesto, opposing the Supreme Court decision of 1954. They vowed "to use all lawful means to bring about a reversal of this decision which is contrary to the Constitution." Accordingly, laws implementing massive resistance to desegregation were enacted in Alabama, Georgia, Louisiana, Mississippi, South Carolina, and Virginia. While the Southern Manifesto did not explicitly call for the use of violence as a means of preventing black pupils from attending schools with white pupils, its impact generated violence.

A federal court ordered officials at the University of Alabama to admit a black student in February 1956. Her appearance on campus was met by mob violence from white students and others who were determined to maintain an all-white student enrollment. She was removed from campus when the rioting flared and was forced to sue for readmission. The university officials responded with permanent expulsion on the grounds that she had made unfair statements about the University of Alabama.

VIOLENT OPPOSITION

On the elementary- and secondary-school levels violence became the accepted means of preventing desegregation. In September 1956 a mob prevented black pupils from enrolling at the public high school in Mansfield, Texas. Mobs demonstrated against school integration in Clinton, Tennessee, and in Sturgis and Clay, Kentucky. In the latter cases it became necessary to deploy the National Guard to protect the black pupils. In the following years, when black parents attempted to enroll their children in schools with previously all-white enrollments, they were met with acts of violence, frequently directed at them by white women. One of the more highly publicized of these events occurred at Central High School in Little Rock, Arkansas, in 1957. The courts had approved a desegregation plan, submitted by the Little Rock School Board, calling for the gradual desegregation of public schools beginning with the admission of nine black students to Central High School. The evening before they were scheduled to enroll, the governor announced that he would dispatch the National Guard to the school because of the possibility of violence. When the first black pupil appeared two days later, she was met by thousands of jeering white citizens, who barred her from entering the building, and by 270 National Guardsmen. Weeks later the National Guardsmen were withdrawn; nine black pupils entered the school, but local citizens forced them to withdraw. Mob violence in Little Rock continued to keep the black pupils from entering the school until the president ordered 1,000 paratroopers to Little Rock and federalized 10,000 members of the Arkansas National Guard to ensure their enrollment. This action represented the first time since Reconstruction that federal troops had been sent into the South to protect the rights of black people. Finally, on September 25, the nine black students entered Central High School. Federal troops remained at Central High School throughout the school year. At the beginning of the following school year the governor of Arkansas ordered all high schools in the city closed for the school year 1958–1959. This was ostensibly done to prevent "impending violence and disorder." When the schools fi-

A group of African American students leaves Central High School under the protection of federal troops.

nally reopened in 1959, black pupils enrolled in both Central High School and another high school, which had previously maintained a policy of admitting only white pupils.

Little Rock was not alone in its policy of massive resistance to integration through the closing of public schools. When desegregation was ordered for the Virginia cities of Norfolk, Charlottesville, and Front Royal, the governor responded by closing the schools involved. In Prince Edward County, Virginia, resistance to desegregation was so strong that the county's public schools were closed from 1959 to 1964.

In the years immediately following 1954, little desegregation of public schools was accomplished. Every September, at the beginning of the school year, one could expect the news wires to carry stories of violence directed toward black pupils. These pupils were frequently required to walk through racist mobs to get to class, and, once in the classroom, they experienced a variety of insults and physical abuse from younger racists.

On the college level, desegregation was not achieved without violence. At both the University of Mississippi and the University of Alabama the admittance of blacks triggered violence by white students. In fact, the admission of one black student to the University of Mississippi in 1962 triggered violence that ended in two deaths and 100 injuries. It was finally necessary to station 12,000 federal troops on the campus to assure the attendance of this student in classes. Federalized National Guardsmen were required to escort two black students to classes at the University of Alabama in 1963.

SEGREGATION STILL THE NORM

By 1960 desegregation of public education was proceeding at a slow pace, and in the Deep South massive resistance remained an effective answer to the Supreme Court's ruling and to the demands of blacks. Feelings of despair over the school segregation issue were widespread in the black community. The federal government assumed no responsibility for ensuring enforcement of blacks' declared constitutional rights. The responsibility for desegregating schools rested with blacks themselves, and when they sought admission for their children to desegregated schools, it was frequently a long, costly, and complicated court procedure. Segregation and discrimination were still the social norms throughout the South, and all-white southern juries continued to refuse to convict white persons responsible for lynching black people.

In February 1960 four black college students in North Carolina sought service at a lunch counter in a five-and-dime store. When they were denied service, they remained seated. The manager ordered the lunch counter closed, but they remained seated, reading their textbooks. The news of their actions quickly spread throughout the country, and within a few days the "sit-in" movement had spread to fifteen cities in five southern states. Whenever a group of black people appeared at a lunch counter, a mob of southern whites appeared to heckle and jeer them. But the actions of the students inspired many others, black and white, to support them. Because of the determined resistance to desegregation of southern whites and because of the strong determination of blacks to achieve social change in race relations, thousands of white Americans joined forces with the blacks to give birth to the civil rights movement. Black college students organized the Student Non-violent Coordinating Committee (SNCC) to coordinate activities aimed at desegregating places of public accommodation in the South. Peaceful demonstrations, led by college students, occurred in every major city where racial segregation was practiced openly. Thousands of blacks and their white supporters were jailed for violating local segregation laws. The lunch counter demonstrations were accompanied by nationwide economic boycotts of stores that maintained practices of segregation. Within a period of one-and-a-half years it was reported that at least 70,000 people, both black and white, participated in the sit-in movement. More than 3,600 were arrested, and some 141 students and 58 faculty members were expelled by college authorities for their activities. Altogether, one or more establishments in each of 108 southern and border cities had been desegregated because of the sit-ins.

THE IDEA SPREADS

The combined effects of these demonstrations and boycotts forced several of the larger chain stores to abandon practices of segregation in service and discrimination in employment. The example then spread to other areas: "Wade-ins" were held at segregated public beaches, and "kneel-ins" were attempted in segregated churches. Always these demonstrations were peaceful, in keeping with the philosophy of nonviolent direct action. However, in virtually all cases there was violence by white people determined to maintain white supremacy at all costs.

The Interstate Commerce Commission had ruled in 1955 that racial segregation of passengers in buses, waiting rooms, and travel coaches involved in interstate travel violated these passengers' constitutional rights. Nevertheless, individual bus drivers and local law enforcement personnel continued to require blacks to sit separated from white passengers. In February 1961 the director of the Congress of Racial Equality (CORE) announced that members of the organization would test the effectiveness of this ruling by staging a series of "free-

Freedom rides

dom rides" throughout the South. Other civil rights organizations joined this effort, and in May a group of black and white activists started their journey from Washington, DC, to New Orleans, Louisiana. When the bus reached Anniston, Alabama, it was bombed and burned by a mob of local whites, and the group of freedom riders was beaten. In Montgomery, Alabama, the presence of the freedom riders was met with such hostility that it was necessary to dispatch 400 U.S. marshals to keep order.

The freedom riders were jailed, beaten, or both in Alabama, Louisiana, and Mississippi. There were more than a dozen freedom rides in the South, and these rides combined the efforts of the four major civil rights organizations. In addition to CORE and SNCC, the National Association for the Advancement of Colored People (NAACP) and the Southern Christian Leadership Conference (SCLC) participated. The freedom rides involved more than one thousand persons, and the legal expenses they incurred exceeded $300,000. As a result of these activities, the Interstate Commerce Commission issued an order outlawing segregation on all buses and in all terminal facilities.

VOTER REGISTRATION

The civil rights movement appealed to increasingly large numbers of white Americans. Demonstrations protesting all forms of segregation and discrimination were conducted throughout the United States, especially in the South. There were attacks on legally imposed segregation in the South and *de facto* segregation elsewhere and on discriminatory practices throughout the country. There were demonstrations at public libraries, swimming pools, public parks, and seats of municipal government throughout the Deep South and the Border South. Discrimination against black people in voting became a special target for civil rights activists, based on the assumption that once armed with the franchise, blacks would be in a position to elect public officials sympathetic to their demands. The Civil Rights Act of 1960 provided for the appointment of federal voting referees to receive applications to qualify voters if it could be proved that a person had been denied the right to vote because of race. Throughout the South voter registration schools were set up in churches. The response of many white southerners was characteristic of their resistance to change in existing practices. Black churches were bombed and burned. Churches had traditionally been exempt from the tyranny that southern blacks encountered daily, and now it appeared that blacks were not safe even in their houses of worship. Appeals to federal officials were in vain, and the reign of terror continued unabated. Arrests for these activities were rare, for local police officers often supported such activities. Black people and their white supporters remained nonviolent despite daily provocations and beatings.

POLICE RESISTANCE

On occasion one city was selected to be a major target of civil rights demonstrations. SNCC selected Greenwood, Mississippi, as the site of its emancipation centennial campaign, in response to an attempt to assassinate one of its field workers. They organized a massive voter registration campaign and were met by heavily armed police officers with police dogs. When they attempted to escort local Mississippi blacks to register to vote, they were attacked by the police and their dogs. The late Martin Luther King, Jr., selected Birmingham, Alabama, as SCLC's major site of antisegregation demonstrations during the centennial year. Birmingham was one of the most rigidly segregated larger cities in the South, and it was believed that if segregation barriers there could be penetrated, it would make for less difficulty elsewhere. The demonstrators were met in Birmingham by a force of police and firefighters led by a well-known segregationist. Police and firefighters were ordered to use a variety of techniques to curb the demonstrations, including fire hoses, cattle prods, and police dogs. For several days the demonstrators met greater brutality from law enforcement personnel than they had ever encountered previously, and the police and firefighters were supported in their acts by an injunction from a local judge prohibiting protest marches. When the demonstrators defied this injunction, hundreds of them were jailed. The constitutional right of citizens to petition peacefully for redress of grievances was violated, and the Department of Justice issued a statement that it was watching the situation but that it was powerless to act. It was decided by the leaders of the demonstrations that schoolchildren should participate along with adults. They, too, were met by police clubs, dogs, and fire hoses. The pictures of the repressive measures used by the police and firefighters alerted the nation and the world to the extremes that segregationists would resort to in order to maintain white supremacy.

A turning point was reached in Birmingham when following a meeting of the Ku Klux Klan, the home of the brother of the late Martin Luther King, Jr., and the motel that had served as King's headquarters and residence were bombed. Thousands of black demonstrators abandoned the philosophy of nonviolence and took to the streets with bottles and stones. They burned houses and stores and stoned police and passing cars. Before the uprising ended, they had burned a nine-block area of the city. When the demonstrators had requested federal protection from police dogs, fire hoses, and police clubs, the president had announced that no federal agency could act. However, when the blacks stoned white police officers and other citizens, federal troops were dispatched to Alabama within hours. Apparently the latter constituted acts of violence, while the former did not.

THE CIVIL RIGHTS ACT

Demonstrations in many other southern and border cities followed those in Birmingham. Danville, Virginia, and Cambridge, Maryland, were among the most prominent. During the summer of 1963 some 35 homes and churches were bombed or burned, at least 10 people were killed, and more than 20,000 demonstrators were arrested. Thousands of others were shocked by cattle prods, set upon with high-pressure fire hoses, bitten by police dogs, and beaten by police. The summer demonstrations culminated in August, when 250,000 blacks and their white supporters participated in the March on Washington, the largest civil rights demonstration in history. As a direct outgrowth of these demonstrations Congress enacted the Civil Rights Act of 1964. The major provisions of this act are as follows: (1) Sixth-grade education was established as a presumption of literacy for voting purposes; (2) segregation and discrimination in places of public accommodation were outlawed; (3) public facilities (parks, playgrounds, libraries, and so on) were desegregated; (4) the attorney general was authorized to file school desegregation suits; (5) discrimination was outlawed in all federally assisted activities; (6) discrimination by employers or unions with 100 or more employees or members was outlawed; (7) the attorney general was authorized to intervene in private suits in which persons alleged denial of equal protection of the laws under the Fourteenth Amendment.

The leaders of several civil rights organizations, after achieving the victory that this act signaled, decided to concentrate their activities on voter registration and education. They had been urged by the Department of Justice to concentrate on these activities instead of street demonstrations. Consequently, in 1964 the Mississippi Summer Project was organized. Thousands of black and white activists journeyed to Mississippi to engage in activities aimed at improving the status of that state's nearly one million blacks. They concentrated on voter education and registration and on "freedom schools." The activists were subjected to a serious initial setback when three of their volunteers were abducted and murdered by a mob of local racists. Throughout the summer they were subjected to a variety of harassments and abuse. The casualty list was high: By October 21 at least 3 persons had been killed, 80 were beaten, 3 were wounded by gunfire in 35 shootings, more than 35 churches were burned, 35 homes and other buildings were bombed, and more than 1,000 persons had been arrested. In addition, several unsolved murders of local blacks were recorded.

The Civil Rights Act of 1964 contained a provision ensuring blacks the right to vote in all elections. However, when

Voting Rights Act 1965

they attempted to register, a variety of techniques, especially intimidation, kept them from exercising this right. Consequently, the major effort for 1965 was the campaign to ensure the right to vote. Resistance to black voting rights was strong. Several civil rights organizations decided to focus their attention on Alabama, which had been one of the most intransigent in this regard. Attempts to register blacks failed, and a march from Selma to Montgomery was planned to dramatize the plight of that state's black citizens. Thousands of black activists and their white supporters gathered in Selma for the march. Several attempts to march were thwarted by the police, under orders from a local sheriff. Acts of excessive use of force by police were widespread, and these acts motivated additional thousands of citizens, including many members of the clergy, from all over the United States to join the activists in Selma. The march finally materialized but not without violence. Two white activists and one black were killed and scores of others were injured.

The Selma-to-Montgomery march stimulated the Voting Rights Act of 1965, which made it possible for southern blacks to register and vote with little difficulty. It was also the last mass demonstration of the civil rights movement. During the years of peak activity, the civil rights movement enlisted the support of thousands of Americans, both black and white. Its nonviolent, direct-action approach was responsible for many of the changes affecting the status of southern blacks. But its goals and methods were hardly applicable to the problems facing the many blacks in urban slums throughout the country. Thousands of blacks and their white supporters had combined for what was felt to be the most significant movement for social change in the United States. The issues were clear, and although there were differences on means toward achieving the goals, a coalition of many groups had united to work for a common end: the eradication of segregation and discrimination in American life. To a significant degree they were successful in achieving greater civil rights for blacks, but black Americans remained basically an oppressed underclass of citizens.

still remained

The Paradox of Nonviolence

JAMES COLAIACO

In this article, James Colaiaco addresses an apparent paradox in the nonviolent style of protest advocated by Martin Luther King Jr. and practiced by many black activists in the South during the 1950s and early 1960s. Although King and those involved in the protests were themselves dedicated to nonviolence, their protests were most successful when they provoked violent reactions from police or white spectators. Colaiaco notes that King was often criticized in his day for provoking violence, but he argues that King and others engaged in nonviolent direct action were responsible only for bringing the violence of a racist society to the surface. James Colaiaco is a member of the faculty of New York University's general studies program.

W hen the definitive history of the American civil rights movement is eventually written, one of the central themes will be that Martin Luther King, Jr. ranks among the greatest political strategists of all time. During the decade of 1955 to 1965, America was the scene of a social revolution that transformed the politics of the entire nation. King organized an army of nonviolent blacks that succeeded in exposing the evils of white racism and overthrowing the legal system of segregation that had prevailed for generations in the South. King's method of militant nonviolent direct action, inspired by the achievement of Mohandas K. Gandhi in India, disrupted the segregationist order by means of marches, mass demonstrations, sit-ins, boycotts and, whenever necessary, civil disobedience. In the short span of ten years more was accomplished than in the previous one hundred, including the en-

Excerpted from "Martin Luther King Jr. and the Paradox of Nonviolent Direct Action," by James Colaiaco, *Martin Luther King Jr. and the Civil Rights Movement*, edited by David Garrow (Brooklyn: Carlson Publishing, 1989). Copyright © 1989 by Carlson Publishing. Reprinted with permission.

actment of the Civil Rights Act of 1964 and the Voting Rights Act of 1965. While King was not the first to employ the nonviolent method in an attempt to resolve the race problem in America, he was the most successful in mobilizing masses of blacks to protest nonviolently for the fulfillment of their basic civil rights.

KING CRITICIZED FOR VIOLENCE

Although dedicated to nonviolence, King drew much criticism because his protest campaigns often were accompanied by violence. In the wake of the successful Birmingham campaign in 1963, journalist Reese Cleghorn wrote that King knew well that "the 'peaceful demonstrations' he organized would bring, at the very least, tough repressive measures by the police. And although he hoped his followers would not respond with violence—he has always stressed a nonviolent philosophy—that was a risk he was prepared to take." Although *Time* magazine chose King as "Man of the Year" in 1964, its feature article contained the following observation: "King preaches endlessly about nonviolence, but his protest movements often lead to violence." When King was awarded the Nobel Peace Prize in December 1964, the *U.S. News & World Report,* in an article entitled "Man of Conflict Wins a Peace Prize," remarked that many Americans believed it "extraordinary that this prize should go to a man whose fame is based upon his battle for civil rights for Negroes—and whose activities often led to violence." In an April 1965 article in the conservative *National Review,* entitled "The Violence of Nonviolence," Frank Meyer attacked what he regarded as the "violent essence" of King's method. He charged that King's campaigns depended upon "the provocation of violence" and a "violent assault upon representative, constitutional government."

Such criticism persisted throughout King's public career. In another *National Review* article, published shortly after King announced plans for a spring 1968 Poor People's Campaign, involving massive civil disobedience in the nation's capital, Meyer assailed what he termed King's "insurrectionary methods," and solemnly warned of impending "anarchy." Another critic, Lionel Lokos, in a book assessing King shortly after his assassination in 1968, charged that King's success depended upon both the threat and the provocation of violence, and argued that he left his nation "a legacy of lawlessness." Lokos concluded: "It has often been remarked that while Martin Luther King himself was virtually Nonviolence on a Pedestal, violence somehow never seemed far behind him." Even staunch supporters of King conceded that his success was largely dependent upon the provocation of violence. Civil rights activist Jan Howard, a participant in the Selma voting-rights campaign in 1965, maintained that although dedicated to nonviolence as a means of action, the civil rights movement needed violence to sustain it. Historian Howard Zinn also admitted that civil rights were often won at the price of violence, but he contended that the degree of violence resulting from protests was insignificant compared to the justice achieved.

THE STRATEGY OF NONVIOLENCE

The controversy over King's method arose from the paradox inherent in the strategy of nonviolent protest. Although King repeatedly preached that violence was immoral, his critics were correct in noting that his nonviolent method was most successful when it provoked violence from defenders of the racist order. In a revealing article for the *Saturday Review,* written during the Selma protest, King articulated the strategy of a successful nonviolent direct action campaign:

1. Nonviolent demonstrators go into the streets to exercise their constitutional rights.
2. Racists resist by unleashing violence against them.
3. Americans of conscience in the name of decency demand federal intervention and legislation.
4. The Administration, under mass pressure, initiates measures of immediate intervention and remedial legislation.

King's critics quoted the above scenario as an example of self-incrimination. They were surprised indeed to find King admitting that nonviolence draws its strength as a technique from the violent reactions of opponents. King and his followers always hoped to achieve their goals peacefully; but since the racist community was usually unyielding, civil rights protesters found that when they used nonviolent soul force, they often were met by physical force. Nevertheless, they were prepared to endure the violence they provoked rather than inflict physical injury upon their opponents. Racists con-

Painful Lessons

A key part of the civil rights struggles involved the techniques of passive resistance and civil disobedience, which required black people to remain calm and collected while subjected to abuse from white citizens and police officers. In the following excerpt from his collection The Least You Need to Know, *Lee Martin describes what it was like to assist, as a white teenager, in this training.*

Three nights a week, when I was seventeen, my father took me downtown and made me shout "monkey," and "nigger," and "coon." He made me shout these things, he said, because he loved me. "Put your heart into it," he told me whenever my voice would falter. "Go on. Get with it. Give it everything you've got."

It was 1960, a touch-and-go time in Nashville. An activist named James Lawson was organizing students from the black colleges, and, because my father sold greeting cards to black-owned variety stores, he had gotten word of the lunch counter sit-ins that were about to get underway. He had decided to hook up with the integration movement because he couldn't resist the drama of it. "This is history," he said to me one night. "The world is going to change, Ed, and someday you'll be able to say you were part of it."

tended that the black protesters should be blamed because their actions precipitated violence and disturbed law and order. Until the protesters arrived, the racists lamented, peace reigned in the community. But this argument rests on the erroneous assumption that the absence of overt conflict in a community means justice is present. The purpose of King's nonviolent direct-action campaigns was to compel racist communities to reveal their injustice and brutality, and to compel

He had volunteered my services as well because he knew I was at an age when it would be difficult for me to stand up for right, and he wanted me to get a head start on being a man of conscience and principle.

Our job was to prepare the students for the abuse they were sure to get. So, on those nights, in classrooms at Fisk University, we stood over the young men and women, and did our best to make their lives sad. My father was a handsome man with wavy hair and long, black eyelashes. He had a friendly smile and a winning way about him, but when he started his taunting, his face would go hard with loathing.

"Get the niggers," he would shout. "Let's get these monkeys out of here."

At his urging, I would join in. "Nigger," I would say, and my jaw and lips would tighten with the word.

We would pick at the students' hair. We would shove at them and pull them down to the floor.

When the workshop leader would call our demonstration to a halt, we would help the students up, and brush off their clothes, and laugh a bit, just to remind them that we were playacting. But always there would be heat in their eyes, because, of course, it was all different for them.

Lee Martin, "The Welcome Table," *The Least You Need to Know.* Louisville, KY: Sarabande Books, 1996.

the government, whether local or federal, to institute legislative reform.

NONVIOLENT BUT COERCIVE MEANS

What King's critics often failed to realize was that nonviolent direct action is not a passive, but a militant and essentially coercive means of bringing about social change. At the beginning of his public career, when King was propelled into international fame by his leadership of the Montgomery bus boycott in 1956, he was inclined to stress the importance of converting his racist opponents by reason and love. But after the wave of student sit-ins throughout the South in 1960, and the Freedom Rides in 1961—which forced Southern communities to comply with federal law—King increasingly perceived the coercive essence of nonviolent direct action. As he developed a more realistic view of humanity and the nature of political power, he saw that most racists were compelled rather than converted. Nonviolent direct action was successful in the South because it exerted political, economic and moral pressure upon the segregationist order. It was this coercive element in King's nonviolent method that provoked violence from racists.

Critics of King concentrated upon the violence that his method stirred, giving scant consideration to the violence inflicted upon the victims of racist oppression. In almost every instance, it was the racists who committed the violence, while the nonviolent protesters provided the occasion for the racists to reveal their true nature. In effect, the racists said to the blacks: "For the sake of law and order, you must submit to a social system even though you believe it to be unjust. If you protest, however nonviolently, I will retaliate violently and blame you for provoking me." On the other hand, when the blacks did not protest, their passivity was interpreted to mean that they were content with their subservient condition. For generations, passive blacks had been virtually invisible—to use novelist Ralph Ellison's well-known description. As a result of the nonviolent protests led by Martin Luther King, Jr., blacks were no longer invisible; they literally had thrust themselves upon the national consciousness.

A HIDDEN VIOLENCE IN RACISM

While it is true that the nonviolent protest movement was to a large extent sustained by the violent racist response it generated, one must realize that this violence was intrinsic to the racist social fabric. Such violence was not always apparent. Beneath the calm facade of the segregationist law and order lay the more subtle and often hidden violence of institutional racism. When not overtly subduing its victims with dogs and clubs, a racist society depends upon a latent form of violence, hidden under the guise of law and order. As long as blacks were willing to accept their oppression, they remained victims of a psychological form of violence, one that stripped them of their dignity as human beings. Denied fundamental civil rights, decent housing, and an adequate education, generations of black Americans were broken in spirit by the silent violence of the racist system. But when the nonviolent protesters employed direct action to confront racism, this hidden violence was exposed. King maintained that by resisting, the black man would "force his oppressor to commit his brutality openly—in the light of day—with the rest of the world looking on." The civil rights movement was able to defeat the segregationist order in the South because the violence that it provoked from racists stirred the nation's conscience by making evident the injustice that had always existed, but under the cloak of legitimacy. Each nonviolent protester became a target, magnetizing the hatred of racists and exposing them to public view through the media. Clearly, to blame the nonviolent protesters for the violence that accompanied King's campaigns in the South is a prime example of distorting reality by blaming the victims.

Attempts to Thwart Desegregation

ANTHONY LEWIS AND THE *NEW YORK TIMES*

In this piece, published in 1964, *New York Times* writer Anthony Lewis argues that one of the remarkable obstacles to the civil rights movement was the corruption of laws by people opposed to desegregation. According to Lewis, the law was abused at all levels in the justice system, by local police forces, by mayors, by voting registrars, by prosecutors, by judges, and even by state supreme courts, legislators, and governors. Nonetheless, Lewis argues, it was eventually federal law, in a series of groundbreaking U.S. Supreme Court cases, which affirmed the civil rights of black Americans. Besides contributing to the *New York Times,* Lewis is a two-time Pulitzer Prize winner and the author of several books.

O n September 19, 1963, twelve Negro residents of Clinton, Louisiana, wrote letters to the mayor and the district attorney requesting the appointment of a bi-racial committee on community relations. They suggested respectfully that such a committee could give "careful consideration of the many problems facing our community" and would help "to avoid civil domestic disturbances of racial tension." One of the writers was a seventy-five-year-old woman, a lifelong resident of the area; another was the husband of the superintendent of the local Negro schools.

The response came on December 3rd, when the twelve Negroes were arrested. The charge was intimidating public officials; bail was set at four thousand dollars each. Somehow the defendants managed to raise the money; but they must await trial.

In Itta Bena, Mississippi, a group of Negroes marched to the

Excerpted from *Portrait of a Decade* by Anthony Lewis and the *New York Times* (New York: Random House, 1964). Copyright © 1964 by the New York Times Company. Reprinted with permission.

home of the deputy sheriff on the night of June 18, 1963, to ask for police protection against harassment of a voter-registration campaign. Fifty-seven were arrested and charged with disturbing the peace. After a night in jail, forty-five of them—all but those less than fifteen years old—were tried by a justice of the peace. They had no lawyer, and no evidence was introduced connecting any individual defendant with illegal action. It took just over an hour for the trial, conviction and sentences. Every man was given a sentence of six months in jail and a fine of five hundred dollars. (The fine amounted to five and one-half months more in jail, at the Mississippi rate of three dollars a day to work off fines, because these impoverished people could not pay.) Each woman was sentenced to four months and two hundred dollars.

To go free while they tried to appeal, the defendants had to produce appeal bonds—fixed at seven hundred and fifty dollars for the men, five hundred dollars for the women. They could not raise that money, and so they were imprisoned, some in the quarters and conditions of chain gangs. Two months later, at the urging of Attorney General Robert F. Kennedy, the National Council of the Churches of Christ in America put up the cash, a New York insurance company wrote a bond, and the defendants were released. At a new trial before a jury they were convicted again. They then appealed to a circuit court. If they lose there, they must go next to the Mississippi Supreme Court. Then they can seek review in the Supreme Court of the United States.

The events in Clinton and Itta Bena were not isolated incidents. Again and again today Negroes in certain parts of the South find themselves caught up in the machinery of the criminal law because of entirely innocent acts—that is, acts that would be innocent anywhere else. A man appeals for help to an official, supposedly his public servant. The next thing he knows he is charged with a crime, arrested, convicted on no evidence of anything that constitutionally can be a crime, held on bail that is difficult or impossible for him to raise, forced to go through a long and frustrating and expensive legal process before someone—probably the Supreme Court—ends the lawless course of law.

The Clinton and Itta Bena cases illustrate a particularly disturbing aspect of southern resistance to change in race relations—corruption of the processes of law. Corruption is not too strong a word; it is used by a gentle man given to understatement, Burke Marshall, the head of the Justice Department's Civil Rights Division, who often gets appeals for help from persons caught up in this kind of southern justice. Not all of the South has forgotten this country's commitment to law; but in Mississippi, Alabama and sections of some other states today, men sworn to exalt the law ruthlessly and cynically misuse it in order to repress the Negro's demand for rights. . . .

A PROBLEM EVERYWHERE

It is important to recognize that defiance of federal law is not just an occasional aberration by an occasional southern police officer. There are places where there is a wholesale perversion of justice, from bottom to top, from police force to supreme court.

The police, for example. On May 8, 1963, a gasoline bomb was thrown into the home of a leading Negro citizen of Holmes County, Mississippi, who headed a voter-registration campaign. The next day he and his common-law wife were arrested and charged with arson of their own home; four student workers were charged with the same crime, and one with obstructing the investigation by photographing the burned house. Eventually the arson charges were dismissed for lack of evidence—there never had been any. By then the man and his wife had gone through a formal marriage ceremony some months earlier. But the local grand jury that looked into the fire indicted them for unlawful cohabitation. Although they were advised that this charge could not legally apply so far back in time, they decided it would be easier to plead guilty and pay a hundred-dollar fine.

And mayors. In Ruleville, Mississippi, on August 6, 1963, Mayor Charles Dorrough arrested three Negro student voting workers because they were accompanying frightened local Negroes to the polls. The mayor was acting in the capacity of police chief, and the formal charge he placed was conspiracy to commit an unstated offense. The students were taken to the town hall, tried by the mayor in his capacity as police magistrate, convicted, given a sentence of thirty days and a fine of one-hundred dollars each. At the "trial" the mayor commented that there was no need to take any testimony, since everyone knew what had happened. The cases were then appealed.

And voting registrars. Among others there is the story . . . of John Hardy—the student who was pistol-whipped by the registrar when he tried to help two Negroes register in Walthall County, Mississippi.

And prosecutors. In Americus, Georgia, on August 8, 1963, four student civil-rights workers, white and Negro, were charged with "insurrection" under a Georgia statute that the Supreme Court had held unconstitutional in 1937. Because this offense was punishable by death, they were denied bail. After they had been in jail two months, the prosecutor, Stephen Pace, stated frankly that he had brought the charge in the hope not of obtaining constitutional convictions but of discouraging civil-rights activities. He said: "The basic reason for bringing these charges was to deny the defendants, or ask the court to deny them, bond. We were in hopes that by holding these men, we would be able to talk to their lawyers and talk to their people and convince them that this type of activity is not the right way to go about it." The defendants stayed in jail until a federal court ordered them released in January, 1964.

And judges. Judge Durwood T. Pye of Atlanta conducted a series of trials in 1963 and 1964 of persons charged with trespass for sit-in demonstrations. He sentenced Ashton Jones, a sixty-seven-year-old white minister from California, to a year and a half in prison and a thousand-dollar fine for helping some Negroes attempt to gain entry to a white church. Then Judge Pye set bail at twenty thousand dollars. The Georgia Supreme Court found that excessive and ordered it reduced to five thousand dollars. Mr. Jones's wife came from California with five thousand dollars, but Judge Pye refused to accept cash, saying only Georgia real estate would do for bond. After Mr. Jones had been in prison seven months, a white Atlanta woman pledged her property for the bail and he was released. . . .

STATE VERSUS FEDERAL JUDGES

Among state supreme courts, Alabama's has a particularly notable record for cynical disregard of federal law. For more than six years it prevented a final ruling on the right of the National Association for the Advancement of Colored People to operate in Alabama—and during that time the N.A.A.C.P. was barred by a "temporary" restraining order from doing business in the state. The ground advanced by the state for ousting the association, that it had not signed a registration form and paid a ten-dollar fee, was found patently unconstitutional by the Supreme Court of the United States in June, 1964. But that was the fourth Supreme Court decision required in the case, and there was no assurance that more may not be needed. Once the Alabama Supreme Court threw out an N.A.A.C.P. appeal on the ground that the wrong form of writ had been used. The U.S. Supreme Court found that ground frivolous, but the Alabama court at first refused to follow the ruling, saying the Supreme Court had been misinformed. A second Supreme Court decision was followed by years of delay, a third warning from Washington and, finally, the first hearing for the N.A.A.C.P. in Alabama. The state supreme court then again refused to pass on the merits of the case, finding this time that the association's lawyers had written their brief in the wrong order. When the case was argued before the U.S. Supreme Court, the lawyer for Alabama found himself embarrassedly unable to explain his own court's decision.

And governors. Again and again such southern governors as George Wallace of Alabama have told their people that federal law need not be obeyed, that decisions of the highest court in the land are not binding, that there is some "legal" way to resist laws one does not like. They have made lawlessness respectable.

And legislators. The legislatures of several southern states attempted to deal with federal measures against racial discrimination by passing transparently invalid statutes purporting to make the exercise of federal rights a state crime. A Mississippi statute declared it a crime to make false statements to any federal official; it was left to state law-enforcement processes to decide what was "false," and the statute added that the assertedly false statement need not be "material" to be punished. When Mississippi officials invoked this statute against two Negroes who testified in the federal courts about voting discrimination, the Justice Department moved to block the state prosecution as an unconstitutional attempt at intimidation.

And all state officials, it must be remembered—legislators and governors and prosecutors and judges—are bound by oath to support the Constitution of the United States. . . .

RIGHTING THE WRONGS

While some areas in the South thus engaged in silent rebellion against federal law, there was no stopping the development of that law in its condemnation of racial discrimination. The Supreme Court did not pause with *Brown v. Board of Education;* inexorably, over the next ten years, its decisions applied the rule against discrimination to more and more aspects of national life.

Within a year of the School decision the Court held that a state could not segregate its parks. Then came libraries, trolleys, buses, golf courses, sports arenas, courtrooms. The Court dealt with these cases summarily, usually elaborating no reasons but simply citing the *Brown* case. That drew some criticism from legal scholars: After all, the *Brown* opinion had emphasized the special nature of education and the way children were affected by segregation; what had that to do with adults riding the buses in Montgomery, Alabama? But it soon became evident that *Brown v. Board of Education* rested on something broader than the articulated grounds. The Court was saying that for a state to segregate human beings by color was inherently invidious, wherever done.

The White Liberal's Retreat from the Cause

MURRAY FRIEDMAN

In this piece, originally published in the *Atlantic Monthly* in 1963, Murray Friedman examines what he calls the white liberal's retreat from the civil rights movement. According to Friedman, although white liberals had been strong supporters of desegregation, the violent reactions of white racists in the South to desegregation convinced many white liberals to be content with a slower pace of integration. Furthermore, Friedman says, as more and more impoverished blacks moved to northern cities, white liberals there had to confront unsettling class and cultural differences that contributed to their retreat from civil rights ideals. Friedman is the director of the Myer and Rosaline Feinstein Center for American Jewish History at Temple University and a former vice chairman of the United States Civil Rights Commission.

In the forties and fifties, liberals, intellectuals, and many middle–class whites came to believe that the elimination of segregation was the central domestic problem in our country. There was general agreement outside the South that once this was accomplished a host of social, political, and economic problems involving the Negro would disappear and he would finally be able to take his place as an equal partner in American life. When the U.S. Supreme Court handed down its momentous decision in 1954 banning segregation in the public schools, a high–water mark in the alliance of the liberal white and the Negro was reached. The decision set in motion the civil rights revolution we are experiencing today, in which the Negro, aided by a sympathetic white community, has been seeking entry into areas of American life previously closed to him.

In the eight and a half years that have elapsed, a reaction to desegregation and to militant efforts by Negroes to achieve it has emerged among many of those who greeted the High Court decision so enthusiastically. These second thoughts have developed as a result of the pain and turmoil involved in making what proved to be difficult social adjustments. In some measure, too, historical anxieties about and antipathy to the Negro have reasserted themselves. Such a retreat or pullback on the part of liberal whites (including many conservatives who are liberal on race issues) has important consequences for civil rights progress.

MORE WILLING TO ACCEPT SLOW CHANGE

One of the indications of this retreat appeared following the wave of resistance that swept through the South after the 1954 decision. Northern liberals expected opposition, but when violence developed in Little Rock, Clinton, and other parts of the South and public schools were closed, they were startled by the extent of the upheaval. Gallup Polls have shown, as Charles Stember has noted in his recent study, *Education and Attitude Change,* a shift in attitude in 1957 among better-educated whites. Increasingly, they have been willing to accept a slower and smaller amount of desegregation in the South.

This mood was reflected by President Eisenhower at press conferences, where he sidestepped expressing an opinion on the decision itself and cautioned that change must first come about in the hearts and minds of men. It is found in the hesitation of the Kennedy Administration (which has been far better on civil rights than its predecessor) to introduce new civil rights legislation and in the efforts of the President to find a national consensus on racial issues.

While Northern opinion has firmly rejected violence and outright defiance of federal court decisions on desegregation, as demonstrated in Mississippi, it has accepted token integration, the device Southerners have skillfully fashioned to avoid the consequences of integration. Apart from indignant Negroes who have reacted with sit-ins and other direct-action efforts, few voices have been raised against token integration, in spite of the fact that less than 8 percent of Negro children in the South are attending desegregated schools, less than one percent if we exclude border areas such as Washington, D.C., and Baltimore. Northern opinion was satisfied with progress made when Atlanta, Dallas, and a few more cities admitted a handful of Negro children to white public schools for the first time without violence.

This new understanding of Southern adjustment problems on the part of white supporters of integration also results from certain changes that have taken place in the North. The heavy exodus of Negroes from the South since World War II has, to a large degree, shifted the center of the race problem to the metropolitan areas of the North and West. The Negro is no longer an abstraction to the white liberal but a concrete reality—in many instances, a potential or actual next-door neighbor, a classmate of his child's, a coworker at office or workbench. This confrontation very often points up the gap between the worlds of the Negro and the liberal white.

DIVIDED WORLDS

The white lives in a middle-class society marked by an emphasis and overemphasis on education, aspiration, and advancement. The world of the Negro frequently is the urban slum. It is a world of slum housing and slum living, where violence, family dislocation, and blunted hopes are the norms. (There is, of course, a middle-class Negro community, and it is growing, but most whites have little or no experience with it.) Contact with it produces shock and disgust, as in the description by Marya Mannes of the West Seventies in New York, where she grew up. There are still some nice people there, she writes, but they are lost in a "brown sea of squalor."

Liberal whites are, consequently, caught in the dilemma of believing in equal rights for Negroes and even of working for them, while at the same time attempting to escape from the real and fancied disadvantages of desegregation. In recent years, they have helped put on the books of many cities and states laws banning discrimination in the sale or rental of housing, yet they themselves have been moving to the farthest reaches of the cities and to the suburbs. They have pushed up the enrollment at private and parochial schools, shut their eyes to the widespread practice of gerrymandering of school district lines to avoid integration, and helped to create pressures for separating slow from rapid learners in the public schools, a process which often results in keeping middle-class white children apart from Negro and Puerto Rican youngsters.

I do not want to oversimplify this situation. The movement out of the older areas of cities has always been a form of advancement for Americans. And the pressure for separating slow from rapid learners represents in no small measure concern among middle-class whites that educational excellence be encouraged. Liberals are genuinely worried about what the introduction of unprepared slum children will do to their schools. They are fearful that physical commingling of middle-class children with culturally deprived youngsters will depress the level of the schools serving the former while the latter, unable to keep up because of inadequate preparation and background, will become even more embittered and hostile. The result is that many liberals, while opposed to color lines, are helping to make these lines stronger and tighter.

A COMPLEX SITUATION

It would be easy to dismiss liberal whites as possessing double standards and being as prejudiced as those they criticize, which some, in fact, are; nearer the truth, however, is the fact that they have been confronted with a series of extraordinarily complex problems growing out of the need to adjust to a modern urban society, large numbers of rural Negroes from the South suffering from inferior, segregated educations and other deprivations. The belief of the liberal whites in interracial justice, while morally sound, does not provide a useful guide for dealing with this situation.

To add to his dilemma, the liberal white is increasingly uneasy about the nature and consequences of the Negro revolt. Out of the bitterness and want that have been the lot of the Negro in our society has come a civil rights revolution whose explosive power worries and even frightens those people who traditionally have been sympathetic to the Negro. The N.A.A.C.P. and the Urban League were fashioned early in the century by a coalition of whites and Negroes to change old and create new law on civil rights and help adapt the Negro to his new urban environment. These essentially middle-class techniques of social action are now labeled too slow by newer Negro (and some white) "direct actionists," who have turned to sit-ins and boycotts in the North as well as in the South, "buy Black" campaigns, and strident demands by Negro leaders that Negroes be elected or appointed to office on a frankly racial basis. There has also been a growth in the Negro nationalist movement.

SHARP DISAGREEMENTS

Liberals are increasingly resentful of these demands. In testimony before a congressional committee investigating alleged discrimination against Negroes and Puerto Ricans in unions recently, David Dubinsky cried, "I'll be damned if I will support the idea of the professional Negro, the professional Jew, the professional Italian that a man should be a union officer because of his race, color, or creed. He should be an officer on his merits, ability, character." Quite so. But ethnic and religious considerations have long been a factor in public life, partly for practical reasons but also as a means of providing upward mobility for minorities. It is rather late in the game for liberals to hold up this yardstick rigidly to the Negro.

White leaders who have not or who are thought not to have adjusted to the new tempo of racial change have come under bitter attack. (The Chicago *Daily Defender* recently called Dean McSwain of Northwestern University, chairman of the Chicago Mayor's Committee on School Board nominations, "a well-known Negro hater" and charged his committee was "composed of men and women who are little removed from the Ku Klux Klan and White Citizens Council mentality" because they had proposed no Negroes for school board vacancies.) These harsh criticisms, which many white liberals see as making little or no distinction between friends and enemies, have angered many of them.

Involved also in the disenchantment of some liberals with the new Negro is the realization that they are being thrust aside from positions of leadership in the civil rights effort. Having controlled this fight for so long and dictated much of its strategy, the liberals resent being pushed out. Jewish civil rights groups, for example, have always felt a special interest in the Negro. Jews were active in the creation of the N.A.A.C.P.; for many years it has had Jewish presidents. More and more, Negroes are going it alone. Newer, completely Negro-led groups, such as Martin Luther King's Southern Christian Leadership Conference, the Student Non-Violent Coordinating Committee, and A. Philip Randolph's Negro Labor Council have charged or indicated by their actions that white civil rights groups and the more conservative Negro organizations have been moving too slowly or not moving at all. This has produced considerable friction within the civil rights coalition, as evidenced in the bitter debates between Randolph and George Meany of the AFL-CIO [a labor union]. The N.A.A.C.P. has recently added to the tension by leveling charges of racial discrimination against the Jewish leadership of the International Ladies' Garment Workers Union.

JEWISH LEADERSHIP

The attacks upon Jewish civil rights leadership have been still another element in the growing estrangement of liberals from the Negro. A middle-class group with special status fears growing out of their own experiences with discrimination, Jews are worried about Negroes' moving into their neighborhoods, which are often the first to be broken in the Negro advance. They are caught between their belief in interracial justice and a desire to join the middle-class exodus to the suburbs, a desire which has been heightened by evidence of Negro anti-Semitism and the rise of the "black nationalist" movements. Jews, however, continue to remain in the forefront of the civil rights fight; they are often found in the leadership of efforts to stabilize mixed neighborhoods and are usually the first to welcome newly moved-in Negro families.

In the final analysis, a liberal, white, middle-class society wants to have change, but without trouble. And this an aroused Negro community cannot provide, as was demonstrated in the freedom rides crisis. When the first riders went into Anniston and Birmingham, Alabama, in May, 1961, and were initially greeted by violence, there was strong sympathy for them. As the rides continued, however, the public mood shifted to apprehension.

Attorney General Robert Kennedy called for a cooling-off period. The head of the St. Louis Catholic Interracial Council, a veteran of more than twenty years in civil rights work, announced his opposition to the efforts of outsiders to bring about racial change while supporting sit-ins. "Whatever is used that increases racial tension," he concluded, "is not good, per se." By June 21, the Gallup Poll reported that 63 percent of those aware of the rides disapproved of them.

A DANGER TO AVOID

In his concern about avoiding social turmoil in race relations, the liberal white stands in danger of trying to contain the civil rights revolution. He cannot do this, nor would it be wise to do so if he could. It is a revolt well within the American tradition of social protest. Negro militancy, while it undoubtedly presents certain dangers, has accomplished the white liberal's goal of bringing about civil rights advances. Within a year after the first rides, barriers to racially integrated travel in the South largely disappeared. Important social change is rarely accomplished without conflict; moreover, such change in the South has always required pressures from other parts of the country. If the pent-up bitterness of the Negro community is not relieved by the type of gains symbolized in the accomplishments of the freedom rides or the equally successful boycotts to obtain jobs organized by Negro ministers in many Northern cities, it might easily burst out in new and socially irresponsible directions, perhaps in the further growth of the racist, Negro nationalist movements.

Another area of difficulty lies in the rift that has been developed between the white intellectual and the Negro. To no group is the Negro more indebted. It was the sociologists, anthropologists, psychologists, and liberal thinkers and writers who, beginning in the thirties, attacked the myth of the inferiority of Negroes and helped gain wide acceptance for the belief that Negroes should be accorded equal rights and opportunities. One of the major grounds on which the U.S. Supreme Court rested its decision on desegregation was the evidence of social scientists that public school segregation created in the minds of Negro children feelings of inferiority and denied them equal protection of the laws. It is significant that the Supreme Court has increasingly come under attack from critics outside the South for the reasoning used in its desegregation decision, although few challenge the end result of the decision. Lawyers have taken the High Court to task for basing itself "upon the quicksands of social psychology." . . .

THE LESSONS OF HISTORY

While the statement that there has been a pullback on the part of liberal whites will shock many of those who sincerely want to help Negroes obtain full citizenship, the phenomenon is nothing new in American history. It occurred following Civil War Reconstruction, when many of the Negro's staunchest allies retreated or withdrew completely from the civil rights battle. It has been difficult to sustain the effort to bring the Negro into the mainstream of American life in the face of the strains this creates—his cultural and economic shortcomings and the open and covert opposition to integration that exists in all parts of the country. For hostility to according the Negro social equality has been almost as powerful a force in

American life as has been the effort to secure these rights for him. On a trip through the United States in 1831, Tocqueville wrote, "The prejudice of race appears to be stronger in the states that have abolished slavery than in those where it still exists; and nowhere is it as intolerant as in those states where servitude has never been known.". . .

I do not mean to imply that all the moral fervor has gone out of the white liberal's crusade on behalf of the Negro. Many whites have taken part in freedom rides and sit-ins. A pilot experiment has been completed in Philadelphia in which 175 college and graduate students from campuses around the country spent part of their summer vacation tutoring primarily Negro youngsters to overcome school difficulties.

Nevertheless, an issue or series of issues has developed between many liberals and the Negro, the heart of which seems to be this: many liberals are hinting to a restless Negro group that they postpone their most urgent demands because many Negroes are not yet ready to be integrated into a white middle-class society and the social costs, in terms of conflict, may be too high. One writer in the liberal *New Leader* suggests a new Negro strategy of disengagement to repair the damaged communication lines between whites and Negroes. In other words, to the Negro demand for "now," to which the Deep South has replied "never," many liberal whites are increasingly responding "later." But the Negro will accept nothing short of first-class citizenship, now. It will call for a great deal of patience and understanding among those who make up the civil rights coalition if racial progress is not to be seriously jeopardized.

CHAPTER 3

RADICALIZATION AND A CHANGING MOVEMENT

AMERICAN
SOCIAL
MOVEMENTS

The Movement Heads North

MICHAEL L. LEVINE

In this article, Michael L. Levine traces the development of the civil rights movement as it shifted from the Deep South to the cities in the North. Blacks in northern cities, Levine notes, had not benefited from the civil rights battles of the 1950s and early 1960s. For the most part, he says, blacks were still impoverished and lived in racially segregated cities with little reason to expect change anytime soon. In this setting, Levine argues, it is natural that black nationalism, which emphasized the need to develop black power and pride, found such fertile soil. Levine is a historian and a former writer and researcher with the A. Philip Randolph Institute, the national organization of black trade union activists.

Starting in the mid-1960s, a growing number of blacks began to reject the goal of integration and the strategy of nonviolence. New, angry black leaders appeared on the scene, denouncing white Americans, including liberals, as incurable racists with no intention of ever accepting blacks as equals. They believed that the pursuit of integration would require blacks to abandon their own identity to enter an American mainstream that did not really want them. Instead, the new voices asserted, blacks should work together to build their self-pride, their own economy, and their own communities. Finally, they believed blacks must go beyond the two major strategies being used to attack racism: seeking legal redress in the courts and engaging in nonviolent direct action. The legal strategy assumed that the nation's judicial system was basically fair; the direct action strategy assumed that the consciences of whites could be moved. But the new black voices rejected both assumptions, and so many of them—although not all—argued that blacks must "use any means necessary," including violence, to defeat racism.

Many Americans, and especially white liberals, were shocked as a growing number of blacks (although a minority) voiced these views. How, they asked, could blacks express such anger toward American society just when they were making major progress? Wasn't the civil rights movement tearing down the walls of legalized discrimination? Weren't blacks finding greater acceptance in white society? Wasn't the average black improving his or her economic well-being?

There were many reasons for the seeming contradiction between growing progress and growing anger. The same pattern has occurred often in modern history. When long-oppressed groups finally start to win their rights, they often expect to win total victory very quickly; this is known as the "revolution of rising expectations." But when they realize that complete victory will not come immediately, frustration and bitterness set in. Another reason is that many blacks had long believed that the fight for freedom had two parts: the struggle for legal equality, which was fought by the NAACP and the other civil rights organizations; and the struggle to develop self-pride, cultural identity, and black institutions, as expressed by Booker T. Washington and Marcus Garvey. Once major progress had been achieved in the fight for legal equality, it was natural that many blacks would turn to the task of defining and developing themselves. There are many other explanations as well, a large number of them linked to the problems of northern blacks in particular.

PROBLEMS IN THE NORTH

The North was a breeding ground for black nationalism. The victories of the civil rights movement did not greatly change the lives of northern blacks. Jim Crow had never been as strong in the North as in the South; anyway, it had been on the decline in the northern states since the end of World War II. Furthermore, northern blacks had long been free to vote.

But the problems that northern blacks *did* have—including

poverty, unemployment, and poor housing—required a far larger commitment of resources than the War on Poverty provided, and so proved much more difficult to eliminate than Jim Crow and voting discrimination. This caused northern blacks great frustration, leading many of them to question the willingness of even liberal whites to help them. With regard to housing, the federal government sponsored many urban renewal projects after World War II that replaced dilapidated slums with better housing. But often the poor blacks who had lived in the demolished or renovated slum buildings could not afford to live in the new housing. Another urban renewal practice replaced slums with office buildings or other public structures (such as Lincoln Center for the Performing Arts in New York City, which displaced many thousands of slum dwellers). Blacks often commented that "urban renewal equals Negro removal."

In the decades after the war, millions of southern blacks flocked to northern cities. At the same time, millions of middle- and working-class whites left those cities for suburban towns that kept blacks out. Between 1960 and 1970, for example, the black population of the 34 largest U.S. cities increased by 2.9 million, while their white population went down by 1.9 million. And during the same decade, the white population of the suburbs surrounding those 34 cities increased by 12.5 million; in the same suburbs, racial discrimination kept the increase in black population down to 800,000. Many whites moved to the suburbs simply because postwar prosperity made it possible for them to afford their own homes for the first time. But many others were anxious to leave the cities because blacks were moving in. This pattern was known as "white flight." Because the disappearing whites included liberals as well as conservatives, supporters of civil rights as well as opponents, some blacks claimed that their white allies were hypocrites who talked one way but lived another. . . .

UNEMPLOYMENT AND BLACK HOUSEHOLDS

Despite the economic progress made by some blacks during the 1960s, blacks overall lagged far behind whites. In 1969 blacks still earned well under two-thirds of white income. Black unemployment declined but remained nearly double the white rate. Besides, the number of permanently unemployed blacks was growing. As we have seen, many whites left the northern cities as southern blacks poured into them. A large number of companies followed whites into the new suburbs, from which blacks often were unofficially barred. In 1945 nearly 70 percent of all industrial jobs were in the cities; in 1970 the figure was down to 40 percent. As a result, many poor urban blacks could not reach manufacturing jobs. Furthermore, industrial automation—replacing workers with machines—was eliminating many of those jobs. It also created new jobs, but those required more skills than the jobs that were wiped out—skills that poor, uneducated blacks did not have. The consequences were felt mostly by young blacks—the unemployment rate for young nonwhites grew from less than 25 percent in 1960 to 29 percent in 1970. But even worse, a growing number of young blacks—especially those without much education—now had little hope of *ever* finding work.

Black men with little chance of employment often left their families, encouraged by rules that made women and their children ineligible for welfare when a husband or boyfriend lived at home. Many of these unemployed men never got married, because they could not support a family; this left many poor black women without marriage partners. As a consequence, the proportion of nonwhite families headed by a female grew from around 18 percent in 1950 to about 28 percent in 1970. Female-headed households were more likely to be poor than male-headed households—in 1967 the average full-time female black worker earned $63 a week, compared to $90 a week for the typical black male. Therefore, many black families, especially those headed by women, were trapped in poverty with almost no chance to escape. This growing group of blacks would later become known as the inner-city black underclass. This development further dashed the hopes aroused among northern blacks by the civil rights movement—for many of them, things seemed to be getting worse, not better.

ANTIPOVERTY CUTBACKS AND THE VIETNAM WAR

President Johnson's Great Society and War on Poverty programs gave valuable assistance to poor blacks. But not enough funding was provided to make a great difference for most of them. The Office of Economic Opportunity—which ran most antipoverty programs—spent an average of only $70 a year on each poor person. Funding was highest in 1964, the first year of the antipoverty effort. Cutbacks began in 1965, largely because of an increasingly expensive U.S. military effort to prevent a Communist takeover of South Vietnam.

As the war in Southeast Asia escalated, U.S. military presence in Vietnam grew, reaching 500,000 by 1968. Segregation had been eliminated in the armed services, but discrimination continued—in 1967, for example, blacks made up more than 13 percent of the army's enlisted men but only 3.4 percent of its officers. Also, for many reasons blacks were more likely than whites to serve. A major one was that most blacks had no chance to go to college and so were not eligible for the student draft deferments obtained by many whites. As a consequence, blacks were more likely than whites to end up in Vietnam. When they got there, they were more likely than whites to be assigned to combat—20 percent of the draftees in combat were black. Part of the reason was that blacks, who had fewer educational opportunities than whites, scored lower on army tests. That prevented them from getting assigned to desk jobs. But even comparing blacks and whites who scored the same on the tests, blacks were more likely to end up in combat—therefore, racism seems to have been a factor in assigning draftees. For these reasons, more than 22 percent of the army's dead and injured were black as of late 1966. This fueled yet more resentment among blacks.

BLACK POWER

Black anger and disillusionment with American society was bound to make itself felt at the political level. Some of the first symptoms appeared in the South. In 1964 black activists in Mississippi formed the biracial Mississippi Freedom Democratic Party (MFDP) to challenge white racists for control of the regular Mississippi Democratic organization. Led by NAACP state chairman Aaron Henry, grassroots activist Fannie Lou Hamer, white minister Ed King, and others, an MFDP delegation challenged the state's white racist delegates to the Democratic National Convention in August 1964. But President Johnson did not want to offend southern whites in an election year. Backed by most white liberal leaders in the Democratic Party, he agreed to seat only two of the MFDP delegates—and they would be at-large delegates, not members of the Mississippi delegation. The MFDP rejected this arrangement.

President Johnson, Vice President Hubert Humphrey, a long-time civil rights supporter, and other liberal leaders said that to win elections and accomplish anything in politics, compromises were necessary. But many black civil rights activists were angry and began to question the sincerity of their white allies in the civil rights coalition. These liberals, it seemed to them, were more interested in keeping the support of southern white racists than in sticking with civil rights principles. Therefore, some blacks asked, Why not scrap political alliances with these false friends? Why not, instead, force whites to deal seriously with blacks by building up black power outside of the mainstream political system? Since blacks were only 11 percent of the national population and a minority in every state, it was not clear how far this approach could take them. But in March 1966 Stokely Carmichael and other SNCC [Student Nonviolent Coordinating Committee] leaders began an all-black political party in Alabama, officially called the Lowndes County Freedom Organization but also known as the Black Panther Party because of its symbol. It ran an all-black slate of candidates in the county, which was 80 percent black. (They lost as a result of election fraud.)

REJECTING THE GOAL OF INTEGRATION

In May 1966 Carmichael defeated John Lewis for the leadership of SNCC. For some time, Carmichael had been ques-

tioning the value of white alliances, and he had already rejected nonviolence. The following month during a civil rights
march in Mississippi, he began using the slogan "black power."
This quickly became headline news, because everyone sensed
that the slogan reflected a new attitude among some blacks.
"Black power" was a vague term. Some of its supporters said
it simply meant that blacks would now build up their own
communities and institutions and then seek alliances with
whites on better terms. But many black power advocates went
farther, often describing themselves as black nationalists. They
felt that white America could not rid itself of racism, and that
therefore blacks should live as much as possible apart from
whites, instead of trying to integrate into white society. They
advocated self-determination and self-development through
the creation of black political, economic, and cultural institutions. The most extreme black power advocates were black
separatists, who favored the formation of a black nation. Some
black power supporters advocated violence, others did not. But
most rejected integration, and so also rejected the civil rights
coalition of blacks and white liberals. Not surprisingly, SNCC
expelled its last white members in December 1966.

*Stokely Carmichael speaks to a crowd of students at a 1966 Students for a
Democratic Society conference.*

THE SPREAD OF BLACK DISCONTENT

Although born in the Deep South, the cry of black power got its warmest welcome in the northern ghettos, where despair and anger were strongest. Years before Carmichael was born, a Chicago-based black organization called the Nation of Islam was preaching an unorthodox brand of Islam and calling for the creation of a separate black nation. The Nation of Islam was founded in Detroit around 1930 by an Arab merchant, Wadi Farrad. After Farrad died in 1934, Elijah Muhammad—originally named Elijah Poole—became its leader. Muhammad regarded whites as "blue-eyed devils" who had enslaved blacks, the superior race. He claimed that whites had invented Christianity to keep blacks under control by making them meek, obedient, and nonviolent.

The Nation of Islam, Muhammad claimed, would teach blacks to follow the true religion of Allah; to take pride in their superiority over whites; to defend themselves from white violence by striking back if necessary; to build black businesses and strengthen black communities through discipline and hard work; and eventually to carve out a nation from the United States. The Nation of Islam's approach attracted some middle-class blacks; they could imagine themselves as leaders of the new black nation. But the Black Muslims appealed most to the poorest, least educated, and often angriest blacks—those who felt they had no hope of achieving any kind of success and self-respect in a white-dominated world. Those least hopeful about their future were black convicts, and it was in the prisons where the Muslims had their greatest recruiting success.

The most famous prison convert was Malcolm Little, a pimp, thief, and drug dealer who became Malcolm X after his conversion. (The "X" that Malcolm and other Black Muslims used represented their unknown African family names.) Elijah Muhammad regarded Malcolm as his most brilliant follower and appointed him the leader of Harlem's Mosque Number 7 in the early 1950s. A decade later Malcolm brought national attention to the Muslims with his attacks on the southern civil rights movement. He claimed that any blacks who believed whites would accept them as equals were "insane," and he scorned civil rights activists for being nonviolent in a country where violence was the rule.

Malcolm and Elijah Muhammad had a falling out in 1963. After a pilgrimage to Mecca and conversion to orthodox Islam, Malcolm abandoned his sweeping damnation of all whites and formed his own black nationalist organization, the Organization for Afro-American Unity, in March 1964. A man of deep yet controlled and dignified anger, Malcolm was a mesmerizing speaker who expressed the rage of northern blacks better than anyone of his era. Although he was assassinated in 1965 at age 39, apparently on the orders of the Nation of Islam leadership, his *Autobiography of Malcolm X* (1964) would become the bible of most supporters of black power and black nationalism.

NORTHERN RACE RIOTS

Black rage spread far beyond the ranks of the Black Muslims during the middle and late 1960s. The growing dissatisfaction of northern blacks was expressed in various ways. In every year from 1964 through 1968, many northern cities and towns experienced major black riots. These were different from the old race riots in which whites attacked blacks. The riots of the 1960s were begun by blacks and occurred in black neighborhoods. The violence was directed especially at white-owned property and symbols of white authority, such as police personnel and firefighters. As the riots spread through the North, civil rights expressions like "We shall overcome" and "Black and white together" gave way to shouts of "Burn, baby, burn" and "Kill Whitey."

The worst riot of 1964 occurred in Harlem. But that disturbance would seem small compared to the enormous riot in August 1965—a few days after President Johnson signed the Voting Rights Act—in the Watts section of Los Angeles. Over six days, 34 were killed and more than 1,000 injured. Property damage came to $35 million. Some 14,000 National Guardsmen were needed to stop the violence. In 1966 smaller outbreaks erupted in Cleveland, Chicago, Atlanta, and 35 other cities and towns. The summer of 1967 was marked by two huge riots. The worst violence since Watts occurred in Newark, with 23 killed during six days in July 1967. A little more than a week later Detroit erupted. After a week of rioting, 43 were dead and more than 2,000 injured in the largest race riot since the New York City Draft Riots of 1863. Eleven were killed in a Cleveland riot in 1968. In many of the riots, careless gunfire from police and National Guardsmen contributed to the bloodshed.

In the early and mid-1960s, equal rights advocates had felt great optimism over the gains they were making. But partly because of the riots, much of that optimism had changed to anxiety about race relations by the late 1960s. The National Advisory Commission on Civil Disorders, known as the Kerner Commission, investigated the riots. In the panel's 1968 report, the panel found that white racism was their major cause and concluded that America was "moving toward two societies, one black, one white—separate and unequal.". . .

THE BLACK PANTHER PARTY

Some small nationalist groups advocated violent revolution. Founded in 1963, the Revolutionary Action Movement attempted to build a black liberation army, but massive arrests in 1967 put it out of commission. The Republic of New Africa, created in the late 1960s, called for a black nation in the Deep South states; its armed wing was the Black Legion.

But the largest and best-known armed black organization of the late 1960s and 1970s was the Black Panther Party for Self-Defense. It was founded in Oakland, California, in October 1966 by black college students Huey Newton and Bobby Seale to fight police brutality. The Panthers openly carried weapons on the streets. When a group of them entered the California state legislature in 1967 carrying automatic weapons in protest against a gun control bill, the Panthers became national celebrities. The party soon spread across the country, opening chapters in many ghettos (although it had only a few thousand members). Eldridge Cleaver, an ex-convict and author of *Soul on Ice* (1968), a book about the effect of racism on young black men, became its most articulate spokesperson.

The party combined black nationalism with Marxism, calling for black self-determination while praising North Korean Communist leader Kim Il Sung as an outstanding revolutionary and selling copies of *Quotations from Chairman Mao Tse-tung* (also known as the Little Red Book). The Panthers were not antiwhite and in fact welcomed white support. They won a great deal of sympathy from the white student radical movement of late 1960s, which had emerged out of anti–Vietnam War activity on college campuses. This support may have misled the Panthers into believing that many whites endorsed their program. Actually, the campus radicals spoke for only a very small (although very visible) part of the white population.

Local police departments and the Federal Bureau of Investigation (FBI) considered the Black Panthers to be extremely dangerous. These agencies were not fussy about the methods they used against the party, which included infiltrating it with informers and conducting raids; in a Chicago raid, Panther leaders Fred Hampton and Mark Clark were killed, although they had offered no resistance. The police also started shootouts that killed a number of Panthers. Other confrontations with police, however, were apparently begun by the Panthers—not surprisingly for a group that popularized the slogan, "Off the pigs" (kill the police). But whoever was to blame for the violence, one thing was clear: the authorities had much more firepower and many more personnel than did the Panthers. By end of the 1970s, the Panthers had been largely defeated.

Malcolm's Message

JAMES H. CONE

Professor James H. Cone, author of *Martin and Malcolm and America: A Dream or a Nightmare,* argues that Malcolm X had a greater impact on the minds of black Americans than anyone else in the late twentieth century. More than anyone else, Cone says, Malcolm X spoke the "truth," and transformed blackness into something of which African Americans could be proud. Although he was often hated and feared in his day, according to Cone, those who hated and feared Malcolm X misunderstood his message.

No one had a greater impact on the cultural consciousness of African-Americans during the second half of the 20th century than Malcolm X. More than anyone else he revolutionized the black mind, transforming docile Negroes and self-effacing colored people into proud blacks and self-confident African-Americans. Civil rights activists became Black Power militants and declared, "It's nation time." Preachers and religious scholars created a black theology and proclaimed God as liberator and Jesus Christ as black. College and university students demanded and won black studies. Poets, playwrights, musicians, painters and other artists created a new black aesthetics and ardently proclaimed that "black is beautiful."

No area of the African-American community escaped Malcolm's influence. The mainstream black leaders who dismissed him as a rabble-rouser today embrace his cultural philosophy and urge blacks to love themselves first before they even think about loving others. No one loved blacks more than Malcolm nor taught us more about ourselves. Before Malcolm most blacks wanted nothing to do with Africa. But he taught us that "you can't hate the roots of the tree and not hate the tree; you

From "Malcolm X: The Impact of a Cultural Revolutionary," by James H. Cone, *The Christian Century,* December 23–30, 1992. Copyright © 1992 by the Christian Century Foundation. Reprinted with permission.

can't hate your origin and not end up hating yourself; you can't hate Africa and not hate yourself." A simple, profound truth; one that blacks needed (and still need) to hear. And no one said it as effectively as Malcolm X.

EARLY YEARS

Who was Malcolm X? He was born Malcolm Little in Omaha, Nebraska, on May 19, 1925. His father, J. Early Little, was a Baptist preacher and a dedicated organizer for Marcus Garvey's Universal Negro Improvement Association. His mother, M. Louise Norton, also a Garveyite, was a West Indian from Grenada.

The Little family was driven out of Omaha by the Ku Klux Klan before Malcolm reached his first birthday. Another white hate group, called the Black Legion, burned down the Little's house in Lansing, Michigan, during Malcolm's childhood. Malcolm described the experience as "the nightmare in 1929." Soon after, his father was killed, thrown under a street car by the Black Legionnaires, Malcolm reported in his *Autobiography*.

With no husband, without the proceeds of his life insurance policy (the company refused to pay) and faced with constant harassment by the state welfare officials, Louise Little, a very proud woman, broke down under the emotional and economic strain of caring for eight children during the Depression. The Little children became wards of the state. Six of them, including Malcolm, were placed in foster homes. Malcolm's delinquent behavior eventually landed him in a detention home in Mason, Michigan, where he was allowed to attend junior high. He was the only black in his class. Although Malcolm was an outstanding student and extremely popular among his peers, he dropped out of school when his white eighth grade English teacher discouraged him from becoming a lawyer and suggested carpentry as a more "realistic goal for a nigger."

From Michigan, Malcolm journeyed to Boston and then to New York where he became known as "Detroit Red." He was involved in a life of crime—numbers, dope, con games of many kinds and thievery of all sorts, including armed robbery. Malcolm described himself as "one of the most depraved parasitical hustlers" in New York—"nervy and cunning enough to live by my wits, exploiting any prey that presented itself." A few months before he reached his 21st birthday, Malcolm was convicted and sentenced to eight to ten years in a Massachusetts prison for burglary.

In prison Malcolm's life was transformed when he discovered (through the influence of an inmate) the liberating value of education and (through his family) the empowering message of Elijah Muhammad's Nation of Islam. Both gave him what he did not have: self-respect as a black person. For the first time since attending the Garvey meetings with his father, Malcolm was proud to be black and to learn about Africans who "built great empires and civilizations and cultures."

A Transformation

Discovering knowledge through reading raised Malcolm's consciousness. He found out that history had been "whitened" and blacks had been left out. "It's a crime," Malcolm said, expressing his anger, "the lie that has been told to generations of blacks and whites. Little innocent black children born of parents who believed that their race had no history. Little black children seeing, before they could talk, that their parents considered themselves inferior. Innocent little black children growing up, living out their lives, dying of old age—and all their lives ashamed of being black."

Malcolm pledged while in prison to use his intellectual resources to destroy black self-hate and to replace it with black self-esteem. He transformed his prison cell into a hall of learning where he educated himself about "the brainwashed condition of blacks" and the crimes which "the devil white man" had committed against them. He was so engrossed in his studies that he even forgot he was in prison. "In every free moment I had," Malcolm reflected, "if I was not reading in the library, I was reading on my bunk. You couldn't have gotten me out of books with a wedge."

It was also in prison that Malcolm developed his debating skills. Debating, he said, was "like being on a battlefield—with intellectual and philosophical bullets." He became so effective in public speaking that even his opponents had to acknowledge his talent. Martin Luther King, Jr., and other mainstream civil rights leaders refused to appear on the same platform with him. People who did debate him often regretted it. For Malcolm

Malcolm X

there was no place for moderation or disinterested objectivity when one's freedom is at stake. "You can't negotiate upon freedom," he said. "You either fight for it or shut up."

After his release from prison in 1952 Malcolm became a minister in the Nation of Islam and its most effective recruiter and apologist. In June 1954 Elijah Muhammad appointed Malcolm the head minister of the influential Temple Number 7 in Harlem. Speaking regularly in the Temple and at many street-corner rallies, Malcolm told Harlemites that "we are black first and everything else second." "We are not Americans," he said. "We are Africans who happen to be in America. We didn't land on Plymouth Rock. That rock landed on us."

MALCOLM'S MESSAGE

Malcolm's primary audience was the "little black people in the street," the ones at the "bottom of the social heap." His message was harsh and bitter, a "sharp truth" that "cuts" and "causes great pain." "But if you can take the truth," he assured Harlem blacks, "it will cure you and save you from an otherwise certain death." Malcolm told them that they were "zombies," "walking dead people," who had been cut off from any knowledge of their past history. "We have been robbed deaf, dumb and blind to the true knowledge of ourselves." We do not even know our names or our original language. We carry the slavemasters' names and speak their language. We even accepted the slave-masters' religion of Christianity, which teaches us that "black is a curse." How can a people make others treat and respect them as human beings if they are culturally and spiritually dead?

After describing their zombie-like state, Malcolm commanded blacks to "wake up" to "their humanity, to their own worth, and to their cultural heritage." He also told them to "clean up" themselves of drunkenness, profanity, drugs, crime and other moral failings. A resurrected, morally upright black people will be able to "stand up" and "do something for themselves instead of sitting around and waiting for white people to solve our problems and tell us we are free."

Initially, Malcolm's black nationalist message was very unpopular in the African-American community. The media (both white and black) portrayed him as a teacher of hate and a promoter of violence. It was the age of integration, and love and nonviolence were advocated as the only way to achieve it. Most blacks shared Martin Luther King, Jr.'s dream that they would soon enter the mainstream of American society. They really believed that the majority of whites were genuinely sorry for what America had done to blacks and were now ready to right the wrongs and to treat blacks as human beings.

Malcolm did not share the optimism of the civil rights movement and thus found himself speaking to many unsympathetic audiences. He did not mind speaking against the dominant mood of the time as long as he knew that he was speaking the truth. He defined the Nation of Islam as "the religion of naked, undressed truth." "You shall know the truth and the truth shall make you free" was his favorite biblical passage. "If you are afraid to tell truth," he railed at his audience, "you don't deserve freedom." With truth on his side, Malcolm relished the odds that were against him. His task was to wake up "dead Negroes" by revealing to them the truth about America and about themselves.

The enormity of this challenge motivated Malcolm to attack head on the philosophy of Martin King and the civil rights movement. He dismissed the charge that he was teaching hate: "It is the man who has made a slave out of you who is teaching hate." He rejected integration: "An integrated cup of coffee is insufficient pay for 400 years of slave labor." He denounced nonviolence as "the philosophy of a fool": "There is no philosophy more befitting to the white man's tactics for keeping his foot on the black man's neck." He ridiculed King's 1963 "I have a dream" speech: "While King was having a dream, the rest of us Negroes are having a nightmare." He also rejected as inhuman King's command to love the enemy: "It is not possible to love a man whose chief purpose in life is to humiliate you and still be considered a normal human being."

As long as Malcolm stayed in the Black Muslim movement he was not entirely free to speak his own mind. He had to represent Elijah Muhammad, the sole and absolute authority in the Nation of Islam. But in December 1963 Malcolm disobeyed Muhammad and described President Kennedy's assassination as an instance of the "chickens coming home to roost." Muhammad rebuked him and used the incident as an opportunity to silence his star pupil—first for 90 days and then indefinitely. Malcolm soon realized that much more was involved in his silence than what he had said about the Kennedy assassination. Jealousy and envy in Muhammad's family circle were the primary motives behind his silencing, and this meant the ban would never be lifted.

For the sake of black people who needed to hear the message of black self-worth he was so adept in proclaiming, Malcolm reluctantly declared his independence in March 1964. His break with the Black Muslim movement was an important turning point. He was now free to develop his own philosophy of the black freedom struggle.

Malcolm, however, had already begun to show independent thinking in his great "Message to the Grass Roots" speech, given in Detroit three weeks before his silencing. In that speech he endorsed black nationalism as his political philosophy, thereby separating himself not only from the civil rights movement but, more important, from Muhammad, who had defined the Nation as strictly religious and apolitical. Malcolm contrasted "the black revolution" with "the Negro revolution." The black revolution, he said, is "worldwide," and it is "bloody," "hostile" and "knows no compromise." But the so-called Negro revolution is not even a revolution. Malcolm mocked it: "The only revolution in which the goal is loving your enemy is the Negro revolution. It's the only revolution in which the goal is a desegregated lunch counter, a desegregated theater, a desegregated public park, a desegregated public toilet; you can sit down next to white folks on the toilet." He smiled as the audience broke into hearty laughter at this.

BLACK NATIONALISM

After his break with Muhammad, Malcolm developed more fully his cultural and political black nationalist philosophy in a speech titled, "The Ballot or the Bullet." In urging blacks to exercise their constitutional right to vote, he made a move toward King and the civil rights movement. Later he became more explicit: "Dr. King wants the same thing I want—freedom." Malcolm wanted to join the civil rights movement in order to expand it into a human rights movement, thereby internationalizing the black freedom struggle, making it more radical and more militant.

During his period of independence from the Nation of Islam nothing influenced Malcolm more than his travels abroad. He visited countries in the Middle East, Africa and Europe, where he explained the black struggle for justice in the U.S. and linked it with liberation struggles throughout the world. "You can't understand what is going on in Mississippi if you don't know what is going on in the Congo," he told Harlem blacks. "They are both the same. The same interests are at stake."

On February 21, 1965, Malcolm X was shot down by assassins as he started to speak to a crowd of 400 blacks at the Audubon Ballroom in Harlem. He was only 39.

Although dead for nearly 27 years [as of 1992], Malcolm's influence in the African-American community is much greater today than during his lifetime. His most far-reaching impact was among the masses of African-Americans in the ghettos of American cities. He told them, as James Baldwin observed, that "they should be proud of being black and God knows they should be. This is a very important thing to hear in a country that assures you that you should be ashamed of it." Saying what Malcolm meant to her, a Harlemite said: "He taught me that I was more than a Little Black Sambo or kinky hair or nigger."

MALCOLM'S LEGACY

There is a resurgence of interest in Malcolm in every segment of the African-American community, especially among those who were not yet born when he died. His name, words and face adorn T-shirts, buttons and the cover of rap records. His writings, books about him and tapes of his speeches are sold by street vendors, at cultural festivals and in bookstores. Wherever black people gather to talk about their struggle for justice, the ghost of Malcolm's presence is there, reminding us of the strengths and weaknesses of our past and present efforts. The more we reflect on the meaning of Malcolm's life and message the more we realize the greatness of his legacy.

Malcolm was a cultural revolutionary, an artist of the spoken word. Maya Angelou aptly called him "a charismatic speaker who could play an audience as great musicians play instruments." Peter Bailey said he was a "Master Teacher." Alfred Duckett called him "our sage and our saint." In his eulogy Ossie Davis bestowed upon Malcolm the title: "Our Shining Black Prince." For me, Malcolm was a cultural prophet of blackness. African-Americans who are proud to be black should thank Malcolm for creating the cultural space that lets us claim our African heritage.

All Americans owe Malcolm a great debt. He was not a racist, as many misguided observers have claimed. He was an uncompromising truth-teller whose love for his people empowered him to respect all human beings. "I am for truth," he said, "no matter who tells it. I am for justice no matter who is for or against it. I am a human being first and foremost, and as such I am for whoever and whatever benefits humanity as a whole."

Black Power

STOKELY CARMICHAEL

This text was originally delivered as a speech in 1966 by Stokely Carmichael, one of the founders of the Student Nonviolent Coordinating Committee. According to Carmichael, for too long black people accepted the lies white people told them, and black people have to recognize this and change it. As Carmichael sees it, it is obviously white people, not black people, who deserve the blame for the condition in which black people find themselves. Carmichael advocates what he calls black power, which involves achieving greater self-confidence and respect as well as more economic and political control.

This is 1966 and it seems to me that it's "time out" for nice words. It's time black people got together. We have to say things nobody else in this country is willing to say and find the strength internally and from each other to say the things that need to be said. We have to understand the lies this country has spoken about black people and we have to set the record straight. No one else can do that but black people.

I remember when I was in school they used to say, "If you work real hard, if you sweat, if you are ambitious, then you will be successful." I'm here to tell you that if that was true, black people would own this country, because we sweat more than anybody else in this country. We have to say to this country that you have lied to us. We picked your cotton for $2.00 a day, we washed your dishes, we're the porters in your bank and in your building, we are the janitors and the elevator men. We worked hard and all we get is a little pay and a hard way to go from you. We have to talk not only about what's going on here but what this country is doing across the world. When

Excerpted from Stokely Carmichael's "Black Power Speech," June 28, 1966.

we start getting the internal strength to tell them what should be told and to speak the truth as it should be spoken, let them pick the sides and let the chips fall where they may.

Now, about what black people have to do and what has been done to us by white people. If you are born in Lowndes County, Alabama, Swillingchit, Mississippi, or Harlem, New York, and the color of your skin happens to be black you are going to catch it. The only reason we have to get together is the color of our skins. They oppress us because we are black and we are going to use that blackness to get out of the trick bag they put us in. Don't be ashamed of your color.

TRYING TO BE WHITE

A few years ago, white people used to say, "Well, the reason they live in the ghetto is they are stupid, dumb, lazy, unambitious, apathetic, don't care, happy, contented," and the trouble was a whole lot of us believed that junk about ourselves. We were so busy trying to prove to white folks that we were everything they said we weren't that we got so busy being white we forgot what it was to be black. We are going to call our black brother's hand.

Now, after 1960, when we got moving, they couldn't say we were lazy and dumb and apathetic and all that anymore so they got sophisticated and started to play the dozens [a verbal game of insults that are directed at one's family] with us. They called conferences about our mamas and told us that's why we were where we were at. Some people were sitting up there talking with [President Lyndon] Johnson while he was talking about their mamas. I don't play the dozens with white folks. To set the record straight, the reason we are in the bag we are in isn't because of my mama, it's because of what they did to my mama. That's why I'm where I'm at. We have to put the blame where it belongs. The blame does not belong on the oppressed but on the oppressor, and that's where it is going to stay.

Don't let them scare you when you start opening your mouth—speak the truth. Tell them, "Don't blame us because we haven't ever had the chance to do wrong." They made sure that we have been so blocked-in we couldn't move until they said, "Move." Now there are a number of things we have to do. The only thing we own in this country is the color of our skins and we are ashamed of that because they made us ashamed. We have to stop being ashamed of being black. A broad nose, a thick lip and nappy hair is us and we are going to call that beautiful whether they like it or not. We are not going to fry our hair anymore but they can start wearing their hair natural to look like us.

We have to define how we are going to move, not how they say we can move. We have never been able to do that before. Everybody in this country jumps up and says, "I'm a friend of the civil rights movement. I'm a friend of the Negro." We haven't had the chance to say whether or not that man is stabbing us in the back or not. All those people who are calling us friends are nothing but treacherous enemies and we can take care of our enemies but God deliver us from our "friends." The only protection we are going to have is from each other. We have to build a strong base to let them know if they touch one black man driving his wife to the hospital in Los Angeles, or one black man walking down a highway in Mississippi or if they take one black man who has a rebellion and put him in jail and start talking treason, we are going to disrupt this whole country.

We have to say, "Don't play jive and start writing poems after Malcolm [X] is shot." We have to move from the point where the man left off and stop writing poems. We have to start supporting our own movement. If we can spend all that money to send a preacher to a Baptist convention in a Cadillac then we can spend money to support our own movement.

RIOTS AND THE LAW

Now, let's get to what the white press has been calling riots. In the first place don't get confused with the words they use like "anti-white," "hate," "militant" and all that nonsense like "radical" and "riots." What's happening is rebellions not riots and the extremist element is not RAM [Revolutionary Action

Movement]. As a matter of fact RAM is a very reactionary group, reacting against the pressures white people are putting on them. The extremists in this country are the white people who force us to live the way we live. We have to define our own ethic. We don't have to (and don't make any apologies about it) obey any law that we didn't have a part to make, especially if that law was made to keep us where we are. We have the right to break it.

We have to stop apologizing for each other. We must tell our black brothers and sisters who go to college, "Don't take any job for IBM or Wall Street because you aren't doing anything for us. You are helping this country perpetuate its lies about how democracy rises in this country." They have to come back to the community, where they belong and use their skills to help develop us. We have to tell the doctors, "You can't go to college and come back and charge us $5.00 and $10.00 a visit. You have to charge us 50 cents and be thankful you get that." We have to tell our lawyers not to charge us what they charge but to be happy to take a case and plead it free of charge. We have to define success and tell them the food Ralph Bunche [winner of the Nobel Peace Prize in 1950; the first black to win it] eats doesn't feed our hungry stomachs. We have to tell Ralph Bunche the only reason he is up there is so when we yell they can pull him out. We have to do that, nobody else can do that for us.

We have to talk about wars and soldiers and just what that means. A mercenary is a hired killer and any black man serving in this man's army is a black mercenary, nothing else. A mercenary fights for a country for a price but does not enjoy the rights of the country for which he is fighting. A mercenary will go to Vietnam to fight for free elections for the Vietnamese but doesn't have free elections in Alabama, Mississippi, Georgia, Texas, Louisiana, South Carolina and Washington, D.C. A mercenary goes to Vietnam and gets shot fighting for his country and they won't even bury him in his own hometown. He's a mercenary, that's all. We must find the strength so that when they start grabbing us to fight their war we say, "Hell no."

We have to talk about nonviolence among us, so that we don't cut each other on Friday nights and don't destroy each other but move to a point where we appreciate and love each other. That's the nonviolence that has to be talked about. The psychology the man has used on us has turned us against each other. He says nothing about the cutting that goes on Friday night but talk about raising one fingertip towards him and that's when he jumps up. We have to talk about nonviolence among us first.

OUR RESPONSIBILITY

We have to study black history but don't get fooled. You should know who John Hullett is, and Fannie Lou Hamer is, who Lerone Bennett is, who Max Stanford is, who Lawrence Landry is, who May Mallory is and who Robert Williams is. You have to know these people yourselves because you can't read about them in a book or in the press. You have to know what Mr. X said from his own lips not the *Chicago Sun-Times*. That responsibility is ours. The Muslims call themselves Muslims but the press calls them black Muslims. We have to call them Muslims and go to their mosque to find out what they are talking about firsthand and then we can talk about getting together. Don't let that man get up there and tell you, "Oh, you know those Muslims preach nothing but hate. You shouldn't be messing with them." "Yah, I don't mess with them, yah, I know they bad." The man's name is the Honorable Elijah Muhammad and he represents a great section of the black community. Honor him.

We have to go out and find our young blacks who are cutting and shooting each other and tell them they are doing the cutting and shooting to the wrong people. We have to bring them together and spend the time if we are not just shucking and jiving. This is 1966 and my grandmother used to tell me, "The time is far spent." We have to move this year.

There is a psychological war going on in this country and it's whether or not black people are going to be able to use the terms they want about their movement without white people's blessing. We have to tell them we are going to use the term "Black Power" and we are going to define it because Black Power speaks to us. We can't let them project Black Power because they can only project it from white power and we know what white power has done to us. We have to organize ourselves to speak from a position of strength and stop begging people to look kindly upon us. We are going to build a movement in this country based on the color of our skins that is going to free us from our oppressors and we have to do that ourselves.

We have got to understand what is going on in Lowndes County, Alabama [where Carmichael and SNCC ran an all-black party for local election; the party became known as the Black Panthers], what it means, who is in it and what they are doing so if white people steal that election like they do all over this country then the eyes of black people all over this country will be focused there to let them know we are going to take care of business if they mess with us in Lowndes County. That responsibility lies on all of us, not just the civil rights workers and do-gooders.

GETTING WHAT IS FAIR

If we talk about education we have to educate ourselves, not with Hegel or Plato or the missionaries who came to Africa with the Bible and we had the land and when they left we had the Bible and they had the land. We have to tell them the only way anybody eliminates poverty in this country is to give poor people money. You don't have to Headstart, Uplift and Upward-Bound [social aid programs for minorities] them into your culture. Just give us the money you stole from us, that's all. We have to say to people in this country, "We don't really care about you. For us to get better, we don't have to go to white things. We can do it in our own community, ourselves if you didn't steal the resources that belong there." We have to understand the Horatio Alger [author of countless rags-to-riches stories in which poor people succeed through hard work] lie and that the individualist, profit-concept nonsense will never work for us. We have to form cooperatives and use the profits to benefit our community. We can't tolerate their system.

When we form coalitions we must say on what grounds we are going to form them, not white people telling us how to form them. We must build strength and pride amongst ourselves. We must think politically and get power because we are the only people in this country that are powerless. We are the only people who have to protect ourselves from our protectors. We are the only people who want a man called Willis [Benjamin Willis, the superintendent of Chicago schools] removed who is a racist, that have to lie down in the street and beg a racist named Daley [Richard Daley, then-mayor of Chicago] to remove the racist named Willis. We have to build a movement so we can see Daley and say, "Tell Willis to get hat," and by the time we turn around he is gone. That's Black Power.

Everybody in this country is for "Freedom Now" but not everybody is for Black Power because we have got to get rid of some of the people who have white power. We have got to get us some Black Power. We don't control anything but what white people say we can control. We have to be able to smash any political machine in the country that's oppressing us and bring it to its knees. We have to be aware that if we keep growing and multiplying the way we do in ten years all the major cities are going to be ours. We have to know that in Newark, New Jersey, where we are sixty percent of the population, we went along with their stories about integrating and we got absorbed. All we have to show for it is three councilmen who are speaking for them and not for us. We have to organize ourselves to speak for each other. That's Black Power. We have to move to control the economics and politics of our community.

King's Legacy

VERN E. SMITH AND JON MEACHAM

In this article, Vern E. Smith and Jon Meacham, writers at *Newsweek*, explore the legacy of one of the civil rights movement's most famous figures: Martin Luther King Jr. As Smith and Meacham report, thirty years after King's murder there are deep questions and competing visions of King's life and influence. Although King's early target had been racial discrimination, by the time of his death his focus had shifted to chronic poverty and the violence of the Vietnam War. According to Smith and Meacham, King was killed just as his most difficult struggles were about to begin.

The sun was about to set. On Thursday, April 4, 1968, Martin Luther King Jr. had retreated to room 306 of the Lorraine Motel, worrying about a sanitation strike in Memphis and working on his sermon for Sunday. Its title: "Why America May Go to Hell." For King, whose focus had shifted from civil rights to antiwar agitation and populist economics, the Dream was turning dark. He had been depressed, sleeping little and suffering from migraines. In Washington, his plans for a massive Poor People's Campaign were in disarray. In Memphis, King's first march with striking garbagemen had degenerated into riot when young black radicals—not, as in the glory days, angry state troopers—broke King's nonviolent ranks. By 5 P.M. he was hungry and looked forward to a soul-food supper. Always fastidious—a prince of the church—King shaved, splashed on cologne and stepped onto the balcony. He paused; a .30–06 rifle shot slammed King back against the wall, his arms stretched out to his sides as if he were being crucified.

The Passion was complete. As he lay dying, the popular beatification was already under way: Martin Luther King Jr., general and martyr to the greatest moral crusade on the nation's racial battlefield. For most Americans the story seems so straightforward. He was a prophet, our own Gandhi, who led the nation out of the darkness of Jim Crow. His Promised Land was the one he conjured on the steps of the Lincoln Memorial in 1963, a place where his "four little children . . . will not be judged by the color of their skin but by the content of their character."

Now, 30 years after his assassination, that legend is under fresh assault—from King's own family and many of his aging lieutenants. His widow, Coretta, and his heirs are on the front lines of a quiet but pitched battle over the manner of his death and the meaning of his life. They believe James Earl Ray, King's convicted assassin, is innocent and that history has forgotten the real Martin Luther King.

To his family, King was murdered because he was no longer the King of the March on Washington, simply asking for the WHITES ONLY signs to come down. He had grown radical: the King of 1968 was trying to build an interracial coalition to end the war in Vietnam and force major economic reforms—starting with guaranteed annual incomes for all. They charge that the government, probably with Lyndon Johnson's knowledge, feared King might topple the "power structure" and had him assassinated. "The economic movement was why he was killed, frankly," Martin Luther King III told *Newsweek*. "That was frightening to the powers that be." They allege there were political reasons, too. "RFK was considering him as a vice presidential candidate," says Dexter, King's third child. "It's not widely known or discussed, [but] obviously those surveilling him knew of it. They [Kennedy and King] were both considered powerful and influential in terms of bringing together a multiracial coalition."

THE REAL MARTIN LUTHER KING JR.

So who was the real Martin Luther King Jr.—the integrationist preacher of the summer of 1963 or the leftist activist of the spring of 1968? The question is not just academic. Its competing answers shed light on enduring—and urgent—tensions between white and black America over race, class and conspiracy. Most whites want King to be a warm civic memory, an example of the triumph of good over evil. For many African-Americans, however, the sanitizing of King's legacy, and suspicions about a plot to kill him, are yet another example of how larger forces—including the government that so long enslaved them—hijack their history and conspire against them. In a strange way, the war over King's legacy is a sepia-toned O.J. trial, and what you believe depends on who you are.

The Kings, a family still struggling to find its footing personally and politically, are understandably attracted to the grander theories about King's life and death. A government conspiracy to kill a revolutionary on the rise is more commensurate with the greatness of the target than a hater hitting a leader who may have been on the cool side of the mountain. The truth, as always, is more complicated than legend. People who were around Robert Kennedy say it is highly unlikely that there was serious consideration of an RFK-King ticket. "I never heard Kennedy talk about any vice presidential possibilities," says historian Arthur Schlesinger Jr., a Kennedy aide. And though there was almost certainly some kind of small-time plot to kill King, 30 years of speculation and investigation has produced no convincing proof that James Earl Ray was part of a government-led conspiracy.

NEW CHALLENGES

The real King was in fact both radical and pragmatist, prophet and pol. He understood that the clarity of Birmingham and Selma was gone forever, and sensed the tricky racial and political terrain ahead. He knew the country was embarking on a long twilight struggle against poverty and violence—necessarily more diffuse, and more arduous, than the fight against Jim Crow. Jealousies among reformers, always high, would grow even worse; once the target shifted to poverty, it would be tough to replicate the drama that had led to the Civil Rights and Voting Rights Acts in 1964 and '65. "We've got some difficult days ahead," he preached the night before he died.

King was an unlikely martyr to begin with. On Dec. 1, 1955, Rosa Parks declined to give up her seat to a white passenger on a Montgomery bus. King was not quite 27; Coretta had just given birth to their first child, Yolanda. E.D. Nixon, another Montgomery pastor, wanted to host a boycott meeting at King's Dexter Avenue Baptist Church—not because of King but because the church was closest to downtown. When the session ran long, a frustrated minister got up to leave, whispering to King, "This is going to fizzle out. I'm going." King replied, "I would like to go, too, but it's in my church."

He took up the burden, however, and his greatness emerged. He led waves of courageous ordinary people on the streets of the South, from the bus boycott to the Freedom Rides. Behind his public dignity, King was roiled by contradictions and self-doubts. He wasn't interested in money, yet favored silk suits; he summoned a nation to moral reckoning, yet had a weakness for women. He made powerful enemies: J. Edgar Hoover [the director of the FBI] obsessed over King. The FBI, worried that he was under communist influence, wiretapped and harassed the preacher from 1962 until his death.

LOSING INFLUENCE

Hoover may have been overestimating his foe, particularly after 1965. On the streets, the black-power movement thought King's philosophy of nonviolence was out of date. Within the system King fared little better. "The years before '68 were a time when people in Detroit would call us to march for civil rights—come to Chicago, come to L.A.," Jesse Jackson says. "But by the '70s, you had mayors who were doing the work every day." King felt this chill wind in Cleveland, when he campaigned for Carl Stokes, the city's first successful black mayoral candidate. The night Stokes won, King waited in a hotel room for the invitation to join the celebrations. The call never came.

King took the change in climate hard. He told his congregation that "life is a continual story of shattered dreams." "Dr.

King kept saying," John Lewis recalls, "'Where do we go? How do we get there?'" According to David J. Garrow's Pulitzer Prize–winning King biography, *Bearing the Cross,* he had found one answer while reading *Ramparts* magazine at lunch one day in 1967. Coming across photos of napalmed Vietnamese kids, King pushed away his plate of food: "Nothing will ever taste any good for me until I do everything I can to end that war."

Look at this from the eyes of King's family. He is attacking the war and poverty. He is planning to "dislocate" daily life in the capital by bringing the nation's impoverished to camp out in Washington. "He was about to wreck this country," says Hosea Williams, "and they realized they couldn't stop him, and they killed him." But it did not seem that way to Williams— or to King—in real time. The Poor People's Campaign was having so much trouble turning out marchers that one organizer, James Gibson, wrote Williams a terse memo just two weeks before King was to die. "If this is to be a progress report," Gibson told Williams, "I can stop now; there has been none!" The march was to be a model for multiethnic protest— a forerunner to the Rainbow Coalition [an organization founded by Jesse Jackson]. The early returns—and King knew this—were not good. The Southern Christian Leadership Conference (SCLC) was riven as the calculus changed. "I do not think I am at the point where a Mexican can sit in and call strategy on a Steering Committee," one SCLC aide said.

IF KING HAD LIVED

What would have become of King? His lieutenants do not believe he could have kept up the emotional and physical pace of the previous 13 years. They doubt he would have run for office despite speculation about RFK or a presidential bid with Benjamin Spock. Nor do they think he would have pulled a Gandhi and gone to live with the poor. ("Martin would give you anything, but he liked nice things," says one King hand. "He would not have put on sackcloth.")

A more likely fate: pastoring Ebenezer Baptist Church and

using his Nobel platform to speak out—on war and peace, the inner cities, apartheid. King would have stood by liberalism: conservatives who use his words to fight affirmative action are almost certainly wrong. "At the end of his life," says Julian Bond, "King was saying that a nation that has done something *to* the Negro for hundreds of years must now do something *for* him." Had he lived, King might have been the only man with the standing to frame the issue of the ghettos in moral terms. On the other hand, he might have become a man out of time, frustrated by preaching about poverty to a prosperous country.

The fight over King's legacy resonates beyond the small circles of family and historians. To the Malcolm X–saturated hip-hop generation, "by any means necessary" is a better rap beat than "I have a dream." "For kids outside the system, King has no relevancy," says Andre Green, a freshman at Simon's Rock College in Massachusetts. "But for the upwardly mobile, assimilated black youth, King is a hero because he opened the doors." That is true of older African-Americans as well, though there is a rethinking of integration, too. Some black mayors now oppose busing even if it means largely all-African-American schools.

On the last Saturday of his life, sitting in his study at Ebenezer, King fretted and contemplated a fast—a genuine sacrifice for a man who joked about how his collars were growing tighter. He mused about getting out of the full-time movement, maybe becoming president of Morehouse College. Then his spirits started to rise. "He preached himself out of the gloom," says Jackson. "We must turn a minus into a plus," King said, "a stumbling block into a steppingstone—we must go on anyhow." Three decades later, he would want all of us to do the same.

CHAPTER 4

BROADENING
THE AGENDA

AMERICAN
SOCIAL
MOVEMENTS

What Remains to Be Done

In this article, novelist and popular critic Nat Hentoff argues that the
1960s were a time of illusion, during which much was promised but
little was delivered. According to Hentoff, in 1970 black Americans
continued to face considerable discrimination and disadvantage, and
he argues that blacks needed to become more active in the institutions that manage and govern their communities. Hentoff also expressed hope that the younger generation of whites will retain their
ethical responsibility and ally themselves with blacks in the struggle
for civil rights.

M
any laws have been passed in recent years to assure black
Americans their civil rights—their rights to equality of
opportunity in housing, jobs, and education. And yet, as of
1970, how much has actually changed?

The ghettos of American cities are growing at a rate of
more than half a million people a year while living conditions
in those ghettos remain basically unchanged. Forty-three per
cent of the housing in the ghettos is unfit. Infant mortality
among nonwhites in America is 58 per cent higher than
among whites. Unemployment among nonwhites—and that
means mostly black people—has indeed dropped from 7.4 per
cent of the labor force in 1967 to 6.7 per cent in 1968, but it
is still more than twice the rate of unemployment among
whites. Meanwhile, three out of every five new industries are
being built outside the cities, thereby further limiting job possibilities for blacks in urban ghettos.

What of young black Americans? What of their future? Of

those black teenagers who have left school and want to work, fully 25 per cent were without a job in 1968. And even if they had a job, what is their economic future, with limited education, in a society requiring increasingly sophisticated skills?

THE QUALITY OF EDUCATION

If there is any one factor which keeps people poor and without power, it is the quality of education they get. In big city schools throughout America, education for ghetto children has gotten worse in the past ten years. In New York City, for example, considerably less than 5 per cent of the youngsters in predominantly black schools go on to college by contrast with 60 per cent of the young in largely white schools. Let me make this even clearer. More than half of the New York City public school population is nonwhite. But in 1967, out of 30,000 academic diplomas—diplomas which lead to college—only 700 went to black students. The situation is at least as bad in other big cities.

It is no wonder that Julian Bond, a black member of the Georgia State legislature, a young man who has become a national figure and may well hold national political office, says of the present: "What worries me most is that nothing I've done so far politically has really changed the economic conditions of the people in my district. They were very poor when I first ran for office. . . . They are still just as poor."

Considering all the hope which grew from the sit-ins, the Freedom Rides, the 1963 March on Washington, and all those other seeming triumphs in the first stage of "The Movement," the absence of fundamental change for black Americans is all the more depressing, frustrating, and enraging in 1970. But a great deal has been learned in the past ten years. Civil rights laws are not enough; promises are not enough. If there is to be change, it will have to come from black Americans organizing themselves for change. Starting from wherever they are.

Accordingly, there is a rising thrust in the ghettos for blacks to control the institutions in their own communities. The schools have failed so many black children because they have not been accountable to the black community for their failure. And that's why, starting in New York City, and spreading to more and more cities in the country, there is a determined movement for community control of schools. If teachers and principals do not believe that black children can learn, they are to be removed. If textbooks do not speak to the needs and interests of black children, they are to be changed.

Other new lessons are being learned in this battle for community control of the schools. As one mother in the Ocean Hill-Brownsville section of Brooklyn says: "What this school struggle has done is to give us an understanding of how the city works and the necessity of unity of responding as a community." In East Harlem, another neighborhood of New York, community control of the schools has begun, and the local school board reported at the end of last year: "From parties, to conferences on black culture, to political rallies, the community now looks to the schools here as centers of social, cultural, and political activity."

As schools are made accountable to the communities they are supposed to serve, so will other institutions. Health services, for instance. As it is now, black Americans who are poor are treated in distant hospitals by impersonal staffs. They wait for hours in dreary waiting rooms. They are only numbers.

BETTER HEALTH SERVICES

But this is changing. On New York City's Lower East Side, a group of the poor has organized a neighborhood association, and with funds from the United States Public Health Service, they have hired a physician to direct their own new neighborhood clinic. They are in charge, however, of the conditions under which health care will be given. Each patient will have his own doctor; the patient's time schedule will have priority in the making of appointments; and many of the people working in the clinic will be hired from among those living in the neighborhood and will be trained in nursing, physical therapy, and other specialties. Moreover—and this is important in understanding the mood of black Americans now—although the physician-in-charge will do the hiring, each job applicant, including the doctors, will have to pass a committee of community residents. "We want doctors who understand our needs," says one member of the association.

From control of their own schools and their own health clinics, black Americans are also moving toward having a real say in who polices their communities. In Washington, D.C., for instance, the City Council is considering a proposal for elected neighborhood police commissions. Making the police accountable to the community does not mean that local criminals will go unpunished. Quite the opposite will result. The poor are the victims of most crimes, and a neighborhood police commission is going to insist on more responsible and efficient police work than has been customary in ghetto communities. A neighborhood commission will also be able to remove those policemen who regard themselves as colonial overseers and thereby are themselves often a cause of violence. Instead policemen will be hired on the basis of their racial attitudes and their psychological stability.

IMPROVED HOUSING

There are many more ways in which community control is going to grow. Increasingly, black Americans are insisting that they have a say in deciding what kind of housing is built in their neighborhoods, how it is designed. They also want more day care centers for children of women who want to work and control of those day centers.

Yet another development, which will spread in the years ahead, is the concept of the neighborhood corporation. Some already exist, as in Columbus, Ohio, where the 8,000 people in a particular neighborhood elect the directors of that corporation and have a share in it. Money from the federal government is given directly to the corporation in ways the community decides are in its best interest.

Gar Alperovitz of the Kennedy Institute of Politics at Harvard has been deeply involved in this idea and has helped draft legislation by which Congress is likely to make more community corporations possible throughout the country. He further points out that the black community clearly wants to have more of its own businesses; and accordingly, those stores and small factories now owned by outsiders in a black area could be bought by the neighborhood corporation. They would then be operated so that the profits could be plowed back into such community services as day care centers, centers for teenagers, training programs in new careers, improvement of the schools.

There is another reason why the movement toward community control of institutions in the ghetto can become a liberating force for black Americans. To make community control work requires massive sums of money, and the primary source for that money has to be the federal government. Until now, black Americans have not organized themselves into a sufficiently powerful political bloc to ensure that enough of the nation's resources are allocated to the poor. But once black Americans have become directly involved in the schools, in housing, in health services, once they have a sense of their ability to organize themselves on these issues, they will have reason to move in further political directions to make certain they get the funds they need.

It requires working knowledge, moreover, of schools and clinics and housing construction to learn the real amounts of money needed from the federal government; and working knowledge will come with community control. True, the 12 million black Americans are only 11 per cent of the population, but they are strategically situated in the large cities. And if they join together politically, black Americans will be in control of at least a dozen large cities in the next twenty years and will be the deciding vote in other cities. This will mean not only more black mayors and local legislators but more black Americans in state legislatures and in Congress.

An awakened, informed community will insist that the black legislators they elect also be accountable to them. If these officials do not fight for the needs of black Americans, they will not be able to stay in office. And when this bloc of black political strength exists, it will then be possible for black Americans to make political coalitions with white legislators who also recognize the need to provide huge sums of federal money for education, housing, health services, and all those other human needs, by contrast with the present expenditure of so many billions of dollars on weapons of destruction. . . .

YOUNG WHITE AMERICA Baby boomers

Part of the answer [to the uncertainties that face black Americans in the future] is based on the white young. By 1972, the national median age of voters in the United States will be about twenty-six, and the majority of all Americans will be under twenty-one. Obviously, only a minority of the huge numbers of new white voters in the 1970s will have been active on campus during their college years in efforts to bring about a new, much more fully democratic society. But, as a recent study of 860 colleges and universities by the Educational Testing Service has shown, "despite its minority status, the radical student movement is having a very substantial impact" on its contemporaries, on other college students now. "If the movement can be sustained," the study says, "and if ethical responsibility can prevail along with the great freedom sought by the students, the potential of the movement in time for the renewal of American life fairly staggers the imagination."

There is no telling at this time how many of those students will retain their sense of "ethical responsibility" as adults; but it is reasonably likely that most of them will have learned enough, in and out of class, to know that for their own comfort and safety, at the very least, they will have to work with black Americans to reverse their powerlessness and the smouldering frustrations that go with it in the ghettos. For if poverty and powerlessness are not ended, there will be a blight of unprecedented proportions in the cities that will inevitably extend to the suburbs. If only in their own self-interest, this generation of white college young, and those who follow, will recognize the need for alliances with blacks who are already bringing their own forces together. . . .

I started on a gloomy note. Black Americans are bitterly aware of how little has changed for them during the 1960s, despite all the laws, all the speeches, all the singing of *We Shall Overcome*. But they are in movement, organizing themselves to control their own institutions and making certain that they are no longer afflicted with the wholly inadequate education which up to now has kept so many blacks from positions of power. And new generations of black, college-trained intellectuals are going to add their considerable resources to the building of real black power.

Meanwhile, a significant number of today's white college students are markedly different from their predecessors in their degree of understanding of the changes that have to be made locally and nationally. And third, there is the large group of the white lower middle and working class to whom hardly any attention has been paid since the 1930s and who, whatever their prejudices, could be convinced of the value to themselves of fundamental changes in American society.

I cannot predict with certainty that these changes will happen, but despite the bleak present, there have never before been more determined forces for renewing American society than there are now. In the vanguard are the black Americans because they need these changes more and because they have learned beyond any doubt that they cannot wait for others to respond to their needs. They have to take direction over their own lives. And whether the rest of America moves with them or not, they are no longer singing or praying or dancing for liberation. They are organizing for power. And it is on the basis of having accumulated real power that they will be forming alliances with those whites who know that it is in the common interest to end all repression in this country. Since the majority of Americans will be under twenty-one in the 1970s, I expect that by the end of the next ten years, there will be such alliances in considerable strength—alliances of equals.

The 1960s has been essentially a period of illusion. The illusions are over. Black Americans know what has to be done, and so do more and more white Americans—young white Americans.

The Origins of Affirmative Action

ROBERT K. FULLINWIDER

In this piece, Robert K. Fullinwider, a researcher at the School of
Public Affairs at the University of Maryland, traces the development
of affirmative action policy in the United States. According to
Fullinwider, although the term "affirmative action" is nowadays often understood to mean the straightforward use of racial or gender
preferences, the term was not always interpreted in that way. Originally, he argues, affirmative actions were simply those actions that
were designed to root out racism and sexism that lay hidden within
business hiring policies. This kind of affirmative action, he notes,
clearly remains faithful to the 1964 Civil Rights Act, which outlaws
all such discrimination. As he sees it, the shift toward so-called reverse discrimination began in the 1970s, when policy makers began
to speak of setting hiring "goals."

The Civil Rights Act of 1964 set American law and policy four-square against racial discrimination in workplaces,
schoolrooms, and public accommodations. Along with com-
panion legislation against discrimination in housing and voting, the Act swept aside widespread customary practices as old
as the Republic itself. One year later, President Lyndon Johnson's Executive Order 11246 threw the weight of the massive
federal contracting process behind the Title VII prohibition of
employment discrimination. The executive order required that
every federal contractor create and abide by an affirmative action plan as a condition of receiving federal money.

What constituted the racial discrimination that the Civil
Rights Act meant to prohibit? To those who supported the

law, the matter was simple. Everybody knew what discrimination was, they insisted. The sign in the factory window saying "No Colored Apply" was discrimination. The high school's refusal to put blacks on its sports teams was discrimination. The drug store's denying blacks a seat at the lunch counter was discrimination. What could be plainer?

INSTITUTIONALIZED DISCRIMINATION

Soon, however, as the federal courts began to enforce the Civil Rights Act, matters became far less plain. Suppose, for example, that to comply with the law the factory took the sign out of its window but had in place a rule requiring each applicant to supply a recommendation from a current employee. Suppose that another factory abolished its explicit segregation of blacks into maintenance jobs and whites into technical jobs but had in place a rule requiring workers transferring from one job category to another to give up their accumulated seniority. These facially neutral employment practices effectively reproduced the racially exclusionary practices abolished by the law. If all a factory's employees were white, the chance that a black applicant might be able to present the required recommendation was vanishingly small. If a factory's black maintenance workers had to yield years of seniority to transfer to a technical job, few if any could afford to make the sacrifice. In each instance, the factory's rules carried forward the effects of its own past discrimination.

Confronted with case after case like these, the federal courts had to decide how to conceive of practices that locked in place patterns of past exclusion, even though the practices were neutral on their face and not designed with the intent to discriminate. From early on, the courts began to construe such practices as being precluded by the Civil Rights Act in just the same way the sign in the window was precluded. In 1971, the Supreme Court, in *Griggs v. Duke Power Company*, ratified this line of interpretation, holding that a company rule disproportionately excluding blacks counted as discrimination under Title VII *whether or not the company intended such a result*, unless the company could show the practice was necessary to its doing business.

AN IMPORTANT CHANGE

This ruling dramatically broadened the sweep of antidiscrimination law. Now all sorts of work rules and employment practices, from aptitude tests to physical requirements to educational qualifications, were up for grabs. Did black firefighters fail the fire department promotion test in greater proportions than white firefighters? Then the city had better show a demonstrable connection between scoring well on the test and good performance as a promoted firefighter. Did the high school diploma that the factory demanded as a condition of employment exclude more blacks than whites? Then the factory had better show why it needed high school graduates as janitors or laborers. The city and the factory had better show their practices to be *necessary*.

But what constituted "necessity" in such matters? What practices could a court reasonably require a firm or institution to abandon, should those practices exclude blacks disproportionately? In some instances, the answer to this question was easy, in others contentious. As with any reasonableness test, fully informed and well-meaning people could disagree about its application in a particular circumstance.

This evolution in the legal concept of discrimination grounded a further realization. Discrimination need not be the effect of this or that discreet, superficial rule or policy, which a court or government could simply require an employer to abandon. Discrimination could now be seen as built deeply into institutions. Webs of nominally innocent institutional habits and procedures could work to exclude blacks or burden them with special disadvantages. Likewise, they could work to exclude other minorities and women, who were also covered by the Civil Rights Act and beginning to assert their claims through litigation as well. An employer's exclusion of minorities or women might not be the upshot of any single, easily detectable rule or practice that could be isolated and changed;

it might be the effect of many different practices working together. To comply with the law, institutions needed to rethink their operations from the ground up. They needed a mechanism that could shake them out of complacency and habit. That mechanism was affirmative action.

NONPREFERENTIAL AFFIRMATIVE ACTION

The basic idea of affirmative action was simple: motivate firms *to carry on continuous, conscious appraisal of their procedures and rules to detect and eliminate those that excluded minorities and women without appropriate justification.* The mechanism to embody this idea was the ubiquitous affirmative action plan, imposed on all federal contractors by Executive Order 11246. Make a plan, the government told firms in 1972, that includes these steps:

1. Take action to make sure your selection pool is expansive.
2. Given the racial composition of the expanded pool, predict the results over time of your selecting nondiscriminatorily from it. Your prediction constitutes your affirmative action "goals." They give you a benchmark against which to compare actual outcomes.
3. At intervals, compare your actual selections with your "goals." If you are not meeting your goals, then reexamine your rules and procedures to see what is causing the problem.

If your selections match your "goals," the government went on to say, we are not going to look your way. But if your selections fall short of your "goals," we will come to inquire why. If the inquiry shows that your firm has made "good faith" efforts to carry out your affirmative action plan, you will suffer no penalties. After all, your requirement under the law is *not* to select the predicted number of blacks, but *to select without discrimination.* Since the predictions are often based on crude assumptions, there can be many legitimate reasons why the actual outcome wasn't the predicted outcome. But still, we will ask some hard questions: you had better have some very good answers.

This was *nonpreferential affirmative action*. Nonpreferential affirmative action was a *color-conscious, self-monitoring device to aid firms and institutions in achieving nondiscrimination*. And it was also a device enforcers of the law could use to measure compliance.

EXPECTATIONS AS GOALS

The controversy surrounding this version of affirmative action centered on the outcomes that were to be expected in the absence of discrimination. "This predictive aspect of Affirmative Action could be called any number of things," Stanley Pottinger, director of the Office of Civil Rights in the Department of Health, Education, and Welfare, observed in 1975. "They happen to be called goals." Would that they *had* been called other things! "Goals" is a misleading description, given the model of affirmative action set out above. In plain English, goals are things you *aim* at. But in a nonpreferential affirmative action plan, "goals" aren't what you aim at. What you aim at is nondiscriminatory selection. As a *byproduct* of achieving your aim (nondiscriminatory selection), you *expect* a certain number of blacks or women to be selected. If that expectation is disappointed, you are prompted to wonder why and seek an answer.

Had this conception of affirmative action prevailed as the dominant public understanding, much less controversy would have attached to it. But the model had to compete with quite different interpretations. Since institutions were required to adopt something *called* "goals," most people, whether sympathetic or unsympathetic, naturally took the word at face value and construed *goals* as *aims* incumbent on institutions. Government did not help matters here by prescribing rules that seemed to make elimination of gender and minority "underutilization" the first duty of institutions while at the same time disavowing any intent to require institutions to give preferential treatment.

Ordinary citizens could hardly be faulted for failing to see that the government meant, when it said "goals," not-goals.

Nor could critics of affirmative action be greatly faulted for disbelieving the disclaimer of preferential intent. The disclaimer seemed to rest on a morally specious distinction that the Labor Department and other agencies drew between "goals" and "quotas." The government maintained that "goals" (good) are *flexible* aims whereas "quotas" (bad) are *rigid* ones. But for those critics concerned that affirmative action amounted to a policy of coerced proportional representation by race and gender, it did not matter *morally* whether mandated racial and gender preferences were rigid or flexible. Preferences were still preferences. After all, the problem with that sign in the factory window, "No Colored Apply," was not its rigidity. A more flexible sign, "No Colored Apply, More or Less," or "Almost No Colored Apply," would hardly have constituted a moral or legal improvement.

Even on the Pottinger model, affirmative action raised questions that needed forthright and persuasive answers. If government did not look closely at a contractor who was making the numbers but posed some searching and tough questions to the contractor who wasn't, wouldn't this create an incentive for contractors to make sure they were making the numbers, whatever it took? The prudent contractor, concerned about the bottom line, would hardly scruple at employing covert preferences, would he, if that was the price of legal peace? Unfortunately, the answers to these questions were frequently neither forthright nor satisfying to the critics.

PREFERENTIAL AFFIRMATIVE ACTION

The waters of controversy were further muddied by the parallel existence of genuinely *preferential affirmative action*. By the early 1970s, courts had begun ordering some employers to select by the numbers. Moreover, as the decade went along, the government used the threat of litigation to impose genuine hiring goals on several large, high-profile employers. The AT&T Corporation was a case in point. It agreed to a "Model Affirmative Action Plan" requiring it to "recruit without discrimination," but at the same time to achieve, "within a reasonable time, an employee profile, with respect to race and gender in each major job classification, at a pace beyond that which would occur normally." The Model Plan made explicit provision for the use of racial and gender preferences. Whenever the company failed to meet its quarterly "targets" through its ordinary procedures, the Plan required that "selections be made from among any at least basically qualified candidates for promotion and hiring of the group or groups for which the target is not being met," even if there were more senior and more qualified candidates first in line.

In the AT&T case, then, the "goals" were quite undeniably *goals.* They constituted aims the company had to achieve, even by extraordinary measures if necessary. Nonetheless, the Plan offered the usual disclaimer, insisting that its "goals, intermediate targets and time frames" were "neither rigid nor inflexible quotas, but objectives to be pursued by mobilization of available company resources for a 'good faith effort.'" Once again, the effect of this rhetorical strategy was to confirm the critics' view that the whole apparatus of affirmative action was bent to the same aim. If in the AT&T case the standard disclaimer of nondiscriminatory intent was plainly disingenuous, wasn't that proof positive that the government's own disclaimers were equally mendacious?

JUSTIFIED GOALS

As it was, the government had good reason for the plan it imposed on AT&T, whatever the plan's numerical components were called. Consider the especially acute problem that gender discrimination posed at AT&T. Half of the company's 700,000 employees were female, but they were all operators and secretaries. What was notable about AT&T on close inspection was how deeply the concept of "woman's job" and "man's job" was built into everything the company did. The government concluded that any approach short of force-feeding large numbers of women into "men's" occupations would founder on the profound inertial force of AT&T's inherited ways of doing things. So, with its "targets," "goals," and "objectives," the government sought to break open and destroy an entire corporate culture premised on men's and women's separate spheres.

Similar reasoning lay behind the government's strategy in other cases. For example, after nearly a decade of litigation involving the Mississippi and Alabama highway patrols, the federal courts concluded that discrimination was so deeply built into the culture and operations of the two institutions that the only effective remedy was to require them to hire one black trooper for each white trooper hired until the patrols reached a substantial, specified level of racial integration. The effective way to approach the patrols was not to change their cultures in order to get more blacks into them, but to put more blacks into them in order to change their cultures.

REVERSE DISCRIMINATION

By the middle of the 1970s, employers were caught in a dilemma. If they "underutilized" blacks and women on their workforces or in particular job categories, then even their most "innocent"—i.e., facially neutral—practices could ground a legal charge of discrimination that might be difficult to defend against. Litigation was chancy and settling with the government meant meeting its possibly onerous terms. Look at what happened to AT&T—and to many other giants in the airlines, banking, and steel-making industries, to name a few. An employer, concerned to avoid such a fate, could tinker with this or that work practice and still fail substantially to reduce its "underutilization," and thus fail to reduce the jeopardy of government action.

Yet if the employer embraced programs effectively assuring increased utilization of blacks and women, it faced jeopardy on another front: from reverse discrimination lawsuits. When a Kaiser Chemical Corporation plant in Louisiana decided to remedy the complete absence of blacks in its craft jobs by creating its own on-the-job training program and admitting blacks and whites to it on a one-to-one ratio until 35 percent of craft jobs were filled by blacks, the company was hauled into court by an aggrieved white worker.

In a pivotal decision in 1979, the Supreme Court upheld Kaiser's program; and the Equal Employment Opportunity Commission immediately issued rules effectively immunizing employers from reverse discrimination lawsuits where they were acting on the basis of an approved affirmative action plan. These developments were crucial in stabilizing affirmative action in the 1980s and 1990s among America's private employers. Firms could set about changing work practices to bring them in line with the expanded antidiscrimination mandate, and do so with a conscious eye to the numbers. They could adopt the devices best for them in remaking their total operations so as to accommodate blacks and women without fear of litigation whiplash.

By the mid-1980s, then, the basic patterns of affirmative action in employment settled into stability. All federal contractors that underutilized minorities or women had to put in place affirmative action plans containing goals and timetables. The asymmetry of enforcement pressure—threat of government scrutiny for employers who weren't making the numbers and relative immunity from reverse discrimination lawsuits for those who were—undoubtedly sometimes led to the use of racial preferences. More typically, however, the stable legal environment let institutions remake practices and alter routines that had formerly perpetuated discrimination. In special cases, as we have seen, employers used overt racial or gender preferences under court order or consent decree; but the order or decree was always limited in duration. Indeed, AT&T's Model Affirmative Action Plan expired after six years. Even so, the company voluntarily retained most of its features.

CHAPTER 5

THE CLOSE
OF THE
CIVIL RIGHTS
CENTURY

AMERICAN
SOCIAL
MOVEMENTS

The Return of the Right

JAMES OLIVER HORTON AND LOIS E. HORTON

In this article, James Oliver Horton and Lois E. Horton examine the last two decades of the twentieth century. According to them, Ronald Reagan's election as president heralded the beginning of a gradual shift toward the right in American politics. Under Reagan and his successor, George Bush, the authors charge, the civil rights advances of the previous decades suffered serious setbacks. This trend was accompanied, they report, by growing white impatience with black demands. As they see it, with Bill Clinton's election in 1992 a more sympathetic administration took office, but they note that the African American reaction to his tenure was mixed. Lois Horton is a professor of sociology at George Mason University and James Horton is a professor of American studies and history at George Washington University. Together they have written numerous books on the history of blacks in America.

President Ronald Reagan's much-touted "morning in America" was instead a dark time for most African Americans. This former actor presented a credulous nation with the Hollywood version of its story. He managed to assuage uneasiness about cutting benefits to the poor while redistributing resources to the affluent and greatly increasing the budget deficit and national debt. By the end of his second term, Reagan was a figure of nearly mythic proportions. In 1981 he had survived an assassin's bullet, and a year later, he reinforced his image as an unyielding free-market warrior by standing up to, and breaking, the striking air traffic controllers' union. Charging his Democratic predecessor with pessimism, he had reiterated again and again his belief that progress was unlimited in the United States for anyone with initiative and ambition.

The Reagan administration weakened the federal enforcement of civil rights laws, opposed strengthened voting rights for blacks, encouraged local opposition to busing for school integration, and attempted to eliminate the Legal Services Corporation, which provided legal aid to the poor. The Reagan Justice Department attacked the constitutionality of such affirmative-action agreements as those that had increased the number of blacks in the fire and police departments of Detroit, Boston, and New Orleans by filing suit against them in federal court. In the fall of 1983, Reagan fired three members of the federal Civil Rights Commission who opposed his efforts to reverse the advances made by 1960s civil rights laws. Drawing on the image of a fictional "welfare queen" who drove a "welfare Cadillac" and supposedly lived off the generosity of the U.S. social insurance system, Reagan cut social services to the poor. The Aid to Families with Dependent Children (AFDC) program was cut by more than 17 percent, food stamps by more than 14 percent, and community development grants by more than 37 percent; and the training and public employment program called CETA was eliminated. Reagan's tax cuts and business incentives raised the average household income of the top 1 percent of Americans by 75 percent, compared to a 7 percent rise for the 90 percent at the bottom and middle of the society. The percentage of African Americans in poverty rose from more than 30 percent in 1977 to more than 50 percent by 1993, returning to the levels of the 1950s.

A GROWING DIVIDE

The distance between a small group of affluent blacks and the masses of black lower classes, begun during the 1970s, continued to grow during the 1980s. Many middle-class African Americans depended on the federal government for their employment, and the protection of federal civil service laws made them relatively secure. Their progress widened the income gap within black society, as the average yearly income of the top 5 percent of black Americans reached more than $93,000 by 1985, while the bottom 20 percent earned only about $5,000. The vast majority of African Americans agreed with black journalist Carl Rowan when he wrote that Reagan's "administration encourages, subsidizes, and defends racism" and is "brutally hostile to the non-white people of America." African Americans at all income levels steadfastly opposed Reagan's assault on social services and were angered by his use of oblique racial references for political advantage. They were particularly outraged at Reagan's cynical use of race as he showcased a small, but highly visible group of black conservatives who loyally supported his tactics. In 1983, in a move that horrified civil rights advocates, Reagan appointed black conservative Clarence M. Pendleton, Jr., a vigorous opponent of affirmative-action programs, to chair the National Civil Rights Commission. To head the Equal Employment Opportunity Commission, Reagan appointed Clarence Thomas, a black attorney who claimed to be "unalterably opposed to programs that force[d] or even cajole[d] people to hire a certain percentage of minorities."

By the 1980s conservatism had become more sophisticated and better organized. Right-wing scholars such as economists George Gilder and Jude Waninski attacked what they considered the excesses of liberalism and provided the intellectual rationale for Reagan's economic policies. Republicans even enlisted the support of a few outspoken conservative African Americans, who shielded the Reagan administration from charges of racism as it pursued policies detrimental to general black progress. Economist Thomas Sowell of the Hoover Institute at Stanford University; former followers of Martin Luther King, Ralph Abernathy, and Hosea Williams; and former black power advocate Nathan Wright were among the small group of nationally prominent blacks to support the Republican agenda. Such black conservative academics as Shelby Steele and Glenn Loury chastised blacks for failing to take full advantage of opportunities open to them and preached that individual effort could overcome the problems of black Americans without government aid. One irony of the black con-

servatives' rejection of the value of government social programs was that middle-class educated blacks like themselves
were the prime beneficiaries of these programs.

PUBLIC OPINION SHIFTS

By the mid-1980s changing policies were reflected in public
opinion. In 1986 polls showed that 81 percent of white Americans opposed racial preferences in hiring and promotion as a
way of redressing historic racial job discrimination, but almost
60 percent of blacks favored them. Two-thirds of whites opposed reserving places for blacks in colleges where they had
been traditionally excluded, but almost three-quarters of
African Americans supported such measures. Most alarming,
from the standpoint of many black Americans, was the growing number of whites who argued that blacks had an unfair
advantage in hiring, education, and government assistance, and
charged that progressive policies had created a "reverse racism"
that discriminated against whites. The Democratic presidential primaries of 1988 demonstrated both racial progress and
the growing split between blacks and whites in America. Jesse
Jackson, a powerful orator and popular black leader who had
stood with Martin Luther King, Jr., in the civil rights campaign, made a strong showing in his second run for the presidency. Jackson won the presidential primary election in seven
states and garnered nearly 25 percent of the primary vote
(compared to his Democratic rival, Michael Dukakis, who
won 43 percent). Jackson's vote also illustrated blacks' and
whites' differing opinions. He received 92 percent of black
votes but only 17 percent of white votes.

PLAYING ON STEREOTYPES

During the Reagan years, rhetoric and changes in federal policies encouraged racial resentment, and when Reagan's vice
president, George Bush, ran for president in 1988, his campaign played on racial fear and animosity. While Bush insisted
that the country should "leave the tired baggage of bigotry
behind," and said of himself, "There's not a racist bone in my

one of the most vicious campaigns in recent memory

body," his campaign relied heavily on stereotypes of black immorality and crime. Bush used the image of Willie Horton, a black man sentenced to life in prison in Massachusetts, to attack his Democratic opponent, Massachusetts governor Michael Dukakis. Under the state's prison furlough program, Horton had been granted a weekend pass, had escaped to Maryland, and had terrorized a white couple, beating the man and raping the woman repeatedly. The Bush campaign used this tragedy as a weapon against the Democratic candidate, labeling him a "liberal theorist" who cared more about the rights of criminals than about the safety of American families. One Republican-sponsored article appeared in the popular magazine *Reader's Digest* under the title "Getting Away with Murder" and warned that Dukakis would let criminals out of prison to commit more crimes. A flood of attacks branded Dukakis "soft on crime" and Willie Horton's dark menacing face was ubiquitous in campaign ads. Voters were told, "You, your children, your parents, and your friends can have the opportunity to receive a visit from someone like Willie Horton if Mike Dukakis becomes President."

As Richard Nixon had used the call for "law and order" as a code phrase for race and the problems associated in the public mind with black people in the 1970s, the Bush campaign used crime and the name Willie Horton as code words for race. Bush charged Dukakis with being soft on crime, and Horton came to symbolize the evidence. The message was conveyed by implication that only Republicans could save white America from that threat. The oblique racism that had become acceptable to many white Americans during the Reagan presidency became undeniably obvious in the late 1980s, despite Bush's disclaimers. Southern demagogues had used race to unite their white supporters for most of the twentieth century; Reagan's allusions to "welfare queens" had garnered support for cuts in social welfare; and Bush also found race a useful political tool. The Willie Horton campaign strategy was effective, front-runner Dukakis lost ground dramatically, and George Bush was elected to the presidency in 1988. . . .

FRUSTRATION AND RAGE

According to historians John Hope Franklin and Alfred A. Moss, Jr., the "frustration and rage" of urban blacks in the face of a multiplicity of economic and social problems found cultural expression in the new musical forms of rap and hip-hop. In April 1992 a more threatening expression of black alienation was broadcast to American homes when riots erupted in Los Angeles in response to the acquittal of four white policemen who had been videotaped beating a black man named Rodney King after apprehending him in a high-speed car chase. Tensions were heightened by the fact that there were no blacks on the jury in the policemen's lengthy trial. The four days of rioting that erupted in response to this verdict resulted in thirty-eight deaths, four thousand arrests, 3,700 burned-out buildings, damage estimated at five hundred million dollars, and a great deal of conflict between racial and ethnic groups in the multiethnic city. The renewed importance of the issues of race and poverty was apparent that spring as President Bush and presidential candidate Bill Clinton visited Los Angeles in the aftermath of the riots.

By 1992 the United States had experienced twelve consecutive years of conservative Republican presidencies. For most black Americans these had been difficult times of rising poverty and crime rates and shrinking social services, increasing health needs and decreasing health services, and a widening gap between the financial assets of black households and white households. Under these circumstances the rhetoric of William Jefferson Clinton, the Democratic candidate for the presidency that year, had great appeal. Clinton called for greater economic equity, sustainable job growth, and a social service system that would benefit middle- and lower-income Americans. He spoke to African Americans, face to face, in their churches and community organizations, with sincerity and conviction, restoring the hope that had been missing for more than a decade. He promised a diverse presidential cabinet that would represent Americans of all races and include many women. Clinton won the presidency with only 43 percent of the popular vote, but blacks voted for him in overwhelming numbers, with 82 percent casting Democratic ballots. The victory celebration during the inauguration week in January 1993 promised a new era. That week President-elect Bill Clinton and his wife, Hillary, and Vice President-elect Al Gore and his wife, Tipper, sang "We Are the World" with their multiracial, multicultural supporters, and during the inauguration ceremony, black poet Maya Angelou told the excited multitude:

> Lift up your eyes upon
> This day breaking before you.
> Give birth again
> To the dream.

The new president's cabinet met his supporters' expectations. Clinton appointed Latino Henry Cisneros as secretary of housing and urban development, African Americans Ronald Brown as secretary of commerce, Mike Espy as secretary of agriculture, Hazel O'Leary as secretary of energy, Jesse Brown as secretary of veterans affairs, Joycelyn Elders as surgeon general, and a host of other blacks to high-ranking positions in his administration. However, African American reaction to the first Clinton administration was mixed. Clinton was outspoken and supportive of liberal positions on social issues, but his positions on economic issues did not depart dramatically from those of his Republican predecessor. Clinton focused on the need for more police to fight urban crime, promoted programs for bettering community relations with police, and spoke about getting tough with criminals. Yet this focus seemed to ignore the connection between poverty and crime. In 1995 black unemployment remained twice the level of whites'. Though African Americans were likely to be the victims of crime, without programs to expand economic opportunities, the Clinton crime initiative seemed to reinforce conservative assumptions that African Americans were more likely to be criminals. Clinton's political strategy, however, did refocus assumptions about crime by discussing the issue in meetings with members of the black community.

A New Conservatism

During the Reagan/Bush years, many whites had grown increasingly impatient with arguments that stressed the continuing significance of racism in American life. A growing number of whites believed that blacks received unfair advantages and preferential treatment. One poll showed that two-thirds of white Americans believed that most poor blacks were responsible for their own condition. More Americans reported living in integrated neighborhoods than a generation earlier, but stereotypical beliefs persisted about blacks being prone to crime, lacking in ambition, and not as smart as whites. Such attitudes were reinforced by a popular book entitled *The Bell Curve*, published by Richard Herrnstein and Charles Murray in 1994, which claimed to have found important connections between race and intelligence. This controversial study suggested that African Americans were genetically limited and best suited for society's lower-level jobs. Providing an apparently scientific rationale, this study gave conservative policy makers an argument for opposing affirmative-action programs that sought to remedy discrimination in employment or promotions without seeming to be prejudiced. Perhaps, they could argue, African Americans lacked the ability for more demanding positions.

By the mid-1990s political conservatives led by such Republican spokesmen as former presidential candidate Patrick Buchanan had joined such conservative religious leaders as Ralph Reed and his political Christian Coalition to attack affirmative-action programs in colleges and universities, in businesses, and in governmental employment. They believed the role of colleges and universities to be particularly dangerous. One outcome of the modern civil rights movement was exemplified by student demands for the establishment of African American Studies programs and resulted in an effort to rediscover the African American role in the creation of American history and culture. Developments in African American history since the 1970s had led scholars to rethink the central themes of the nation's development, recognizing the centrality of race, ethnicity, class, and eventually gender in shaping the way Americans see themselves and their society. Many of these scholars were inspired by the social activism of the 1960s and 1970s to pursue scholarship that contributed directly to progress in human rights. As their work challenged traditional historical interpretations, it came under attack from political conservatives unwilling to consider any but celebratory European-dominated conceptions of the American past. In the process the debates over historical authority, the legitimacy of historical sources, and revisions of the historical canon became central to the public discussion of such policy issues as affirmative action in education and employment, curriculum revision, social assistance and welfare, and the role of government in a democratic capitalist society.

The New Realities of Race

ROBIN D.G. KELLEY

In this selection, Robin D.G. Kelley argues that recent trends in immigration have changed the meaning of race relations in America.
Since 1965, increasing numbers of nonwhite immigrants, especially
immigrants from Asia, Central America, and Mexico, have been in-
corporated into the American picture, Kelley says, making it impossible to subscribe to a simple black and white view of race relations.
Although there have been some alliances between black Americans
and the new immigrant groups, Kelley reports, there have also been
some notable interethnic tensions. Kelley is a professor of history
and Africana studies at New York University.

America's changing cultural and ethnic landscape not only
calls into question the longstanding (and always false) presumption that the country was divided into two races—black
and white, it transformed the meaning of race relations in
America's inner cities. Before 1965, Jews were probably the
most visible ethnic group with whom urban blacks had contact who did not simply fall into the category of "white." Relations between blacks and Jews in the past had always been
mixed, running the gamut from allies in radical organizations
to economic competitors. Because some Jews owned small retail outlets in African-American communities—largely because anti-Semitism kept them from establishing businesses
elsewhere—blacks and Jews sometimes dealt with each other
on the basis of a consumer/proprietor relationship. In the aftermath of the urban riots of the late sixties, however, most
Jewish merchants sold off their businesses and the few still re-

siding in the ghetto moved out. Except for places like Brooklyn's Crown Heights community, where tensions between blacks (mostly West Indians) and Hasidic Jews erupted in a major riot in 1991, few inner city blacks live in close proximity to Jews.

But as the Jews moved out of the inner city, new groups of immigrants moved in. The most prominent of the post-1965 wave of immigrants settling in or near African-American communities were Asians from Korea, Vietnam, Cambodia, the Philippines and Samoa, and Latinos from Central America, Cuba, Mexico, and the Dominican Republic.

INTERETHNIC CONFLICT

The combination of economic competition, declining opportunities, scarce public resources, and racist attitudes led to a marked increase in interethnic conflict. In South Central Los Angeles, once an all-black community, Latinos made up about one-fourth of the population in 1992. Job and housing competition between Latinos (most of whom are Central American and Mexican immigrants) and African Americans created enormous tensions between these two groups. Black residents, who in the past had been indifferent to immigration, began supporting measures to limit the entry of Latinos into the United States.

On the other hand, Koreans have been singled out by both blacks and Latinos because a handful own retail establishments and rental property in the poorer sections of South Central Los Angeles. African-American and Latino residents believed the federal government favored Korean immigrants by offering them low-interest loans and grants. The fact is, however, that few Korean merchants received federal aid. The majority in Los Angeles and elsewhere ran small family businesses— mainly liquor stores, groceries, discount markets, and specialized shops such as hair care and manicure supply outlets. Often investing what little capital they brought with them from their home country, Koreans relied on family labor and maintained businesses with very low profit margins. Moreover, the idea that Koreans were denying blacks the opportunity to "own their own" businesses ignores the fact that most Korean establishments (particularly liquor stores) were purchased at enormously high prices from African Americans, who in turn had bought these businesses at high prices from Jews fleeing South Central in the late sixties and early seventies.

Last, and perhaps most important, the vast majority of Koreans were neither merchants nor landlords; they were low-wage workers. Nevertheless, blacks and Latinos perceived Koreans as thriving newcomers, backed by a white racist government, taking money and opportunities away from the residents. These perceptions were intensified by the myth that all Asian immigrants were "model minorities," hard-working and successful entrepreneurs who settled comfortably in the United States, and by a general anti-Asian sentiment that had swept the country after the recessions of the seventies and eighties.

But these interethnic tensions were not based entirely on myths. The daily interactions between blacks and Latinos and Korean merchants generated enormous hostility. A common complaint in Los Angeles and elsewhere (most notably, New York) was that Korean merchants treated black and Latino consumers disrespectfully. Fearful of crime, some Korean store owners have been known to follow customers down the aisles, ask to inspect customers' handbags, and refuse entry to young black males who they think looked "suspicious."

A CONTROVERSIAL KILLING

By the early nineties, tensions between African Americans and Korean merchants escalated to the point of violence. In one six-month period in 1991, at least three African Americans and two Koreans were killed as a result of customer/proprietor disputes. The most dramatic encounter was the fatal shooting of fifteen-year-old Latasha Harlins in Los Angeles by Korean grocer Soon Ja Du, which was captured on videotape and played on network news programs throughout the country. The incident began when Du accused Harlins of stealing a $1.79 bottle of orange juice in spite of the fact that she held the bottle in clear view and had not attempted to leave the store. Angered by the accusation, Harlins exchanged harsh words with Du, and they engaged in some mutual shoving. As soon as Harlins struck a final blow and began to walk out of the store, Soon Ja Du pulled out a pistol from behind the counter and shot her in the back of the head.

African Americans were shocked and saddened by the shooting. Harlins's family pointed out that Latasha was an honor student at Compton High School and had no history of trouble. Local organizations called for boycotts of Korean-owned businesses, and tensions between merchants and community residents escalated even further. But black anger over the shooting turned to outrage when Judge Joyce Karlin sentenced Du to five years probation, a five hundred dollar fine, and community service, prompting a long-uttered lament among African Americans that a black person's life was of minimal value in the United States. Insult was added to injury when, five days after Du's sentencing, a black man from nearby Glendale, California, was sentenced to thirty days in jail for beating his dog.

THE LOS ANGELES RIOTS

The combination of interethnic tensions, white racism, and immense poverty exploded on April 29, 1992, when Los Angeles experienced the most widespread and devastating urban uprising in the history of the United States. The spark for the rebellion was a police brutality trial that ended in the acquittal of four officers who had savagely beaten a black motorist named Rodney King thirteen months earlier. Unlike most incidents of police brutality, this one was captured on videotape by George Holliday, a white plumbing company manager. Holliday tried to report the incident to Los Angeles Police Department officials, but he was rebuffed. Instead, he sold the videotape to a local television station and it soon became national news. The entire nation watched King writhe in pain as he absorbed fifty-six blows in a span of eighty-one seconds. In addition to punching, kicking, and whacking King with a wooden baton, police shocked him twice with a high voltage stun gun. When it was all over, King was left with a broken cheekbone, nine skull fractures, a shattered eye socket, and a broken ankle and needed twenty stitches in his face.

For most viewers, regardless of race, the videotape proved beyond a shadow of a doubt that the officers involved in the beating used excessive force. Thus, when the all-white jury handed down a not-guilty verdict on April 29, 1992, African Americans were shocked, saddened, and then very angry. Throughout Los Angeles, from South Central to downtown, groups of black people began to vent their rage. They were soon joined by Latinos and whites who were also shocked by the verdict. But as the violence unfolded, it became very clear that these riots were not just about the injustice meted out to Rodney King. As one black L.A. resident explained, "It wasn't just the Rodney King verdict. It's the whole thing, the shooting of Latasha Harlins and the lack of jail time for that Korean woman." In some neighborhoods, therefore, blacks and Latinos attacked Korean-owned businesses, white motorists, and each other rather than the police. Among the biggest targets were liquor stores, long seen as the cause of many of the black community's woes. And in the midst of chaos, virtually everyone went after property, seizing furniture, appliances, clothes, and most of all, food.

Unlike previous "race riots," the events in Los Angeles were multiethnic and not limited to the predominantly black ghettos. Buildings burned from West Los Angeles and Watts to Koreatown, Long Beach, and Santa Monica. Of the first five thousand people arrested, fifty-two percent were Latino and only thirty-nine percent were African American. When the smoke finally began to clear on May 2, at least fifty-eight people were killed (twenty-six African Americans, eighteen Latinos, ten whites, two Asians, two unknown) and thousands were injured. The fires left more than five thousand buildings destroyed or badly damaged. The estimated property damage totaled a staggering $785 million.

More than any other event, the L.A. uprising dramatized to

the rest of the country the tragic plight of urban America. And because it occurred during a Presidential election year, there was enormous pressure on President George Bush to offer a prompt response. He proposed Operation Weed and Seed, an urban policy that would provide big tax breaks to entrepreneurs willing to invest in inner cities, some limited programs for disadvantaged children, and a massive buildup of the police and criminal justice system. Indeed, the real emphasis was on the "weed" rather than the "seed" component; nearly eighty percent of the proposed $500 million allocation was earmarked for policing. Bush's proposals were severely criticized by liberal black political leaders and scholars. They felt that the "law-and-order" emphasis was misplaced and that giving tax breaks to companies was not enough to attract capital to South Central L.A. Attempts to do the same thing in the past have failed. On the other hand, black elected officials responded to the rebellion by holding meetings and conferences, and by visiting communities damaged by the riots. Established black leaders criticized the Bush administration's proposals but few proposed policies of their own. One exception was Representative Maxine Waters, who tried desperately but failed to get Congress to pass a sweeping and much-needed urban aid bill.

A Gang Proposal

Ironically, one of the clearest and most comprehensive proposals came from leaders of the two largest black street gangs in Los Angeles. After a long and violent rivalry, leaders of the Bloods and the Crips called a truce and drafted a document called "Give Us the Hammer and the Nails and We Will Rebuild the City." The proposal asked for $2 billion to rebuild deteriorating and damaged neighborhoods; $1 billion to establish hospitals and health-care clinics to South Central Los Angeles; $700 million to improve public education and refurbish schools; $20 million in low-interest loans for minority businesses; $6 million to fund a new law enforcement program that would allow ex-gang members, with the proper training, to accompany the LAPD patrols of the community. If these demands were met, the authors promised to rid Los Angeles of drug dealers and provide matching funds for an AIDS research and awareness center. Of course, some of these same gangs were involved in the drug trade themselves, suggesting that their proposal would eliminate an important source of their own revenue. Besides, it is doubtful that the Bloods and the Crips could raise matching funds. In any event, their efforts were to no avail; the mayor and the city council completely ignored the gang members' proposal.

Despite a deluge of plans and proposals, black Los Angeles remained pretty much unchanged in 1994. Two years after the riots, unemployment was still sky high, job opportunities were scarce, and the historic truce between the Crips and the Bloods had begun to unravel locally. Nevertheless, what happened in Los Angeles represented a kind of crossroads for the United States. It vividly called into question the idea that race relations in this country can be viewed as "black and white." It also underscored the extent of desperation in cities generated by the new global economy. The days when jobs were plentiful, even if they were low-wage jobs, are gone. Now America's inner city has an army of permanently unemployed men and women who have little or no hope of living the American Dream. Most keep pushing on. A handful turn to the underground, the illegal economy of bartering stolen goods and drugs. In some neighborhoods, that is all that is left. Meanwhile, the police deal with this tragedy by placing virtually every black person under siege.

POLICE BRUTALITY

Indeed, by the end of the century police harassment and brutality became the leading source of protest for African Americans, irrespective of class. The problem of police use of excessive force was dramatized by a series of high-profile beatings and shootings, including the 1997 assault on Haitian immigrant Abner Louima. New York police officers arrested, handcuffed, beat, and sexually assaulted Louima in the bathroom of a Brooklyn precinct house. After shoving a broken broomstick into Louima's rectum, officer Justin Volpe threatened to kill him if he told anyone about the assault. Louima did press charges, however, which resulted in Volpe's conviction and more investigations into other cases of racism and excessive force in the New York Police Department.

Less than two years later, members of the same NYPD Street Crimes Unit summarily shot to death another black immigrant, twenty-two-year-old street vendor Amadou Diallo. Despite the fact that he was unarmed, had no criminal record, and looked nothing like the alleged suspect in a Bronx rape case, four officers discharged forty-one bullets on him—nineteen of which entered his body. The Diallo killing prompted the largest police brutality protest in New York's history. Tens of thousands of protestors representing the entire spectrum of race, ethnicity, and age blocked the streets around City Hall and engaged in civil disobedience that resulted in hundreds of arrests. Unfortunately, the Diallo killing and Louima beating were just the tip of the iceberg. During the first six months of 1999, for example, literally dozens of others in New York and across the nation were killed or badly beaten by police under dubious circumstances.

The most notable case highlighting racism in the criminal justice system centers around jailed journalist and activist Mumia Abu-Jamal. A former Black Panther party member whose exposés on police misconduct and racial discrimination in Philadelphia won awards and national acclaim, Mumia had been convicted of first-degree murder and sentenced to death for the alleged shooting of a white police officer on December 9, 1981. He had no prior criminal record, despite being subject to FBI surveillance since he was sixteen years old, and the evidence against Mumia was questionable, to say the least. An international movement, endorsed by many leading celebrities, lawyers, and social justice activists, arose demanding that he receive a new trial. A documentary film entitled *A Case for Reasonable Doubt* revealed a pattern of illegal behavior on the part of the Philadelphia police department, including suppressing evidence, intimidating witnesses, and paying off and threatening individuals to give false testimony, among other things. Even the secretary-general of Amnesty International expressed concern in a 1997 statement that "Mumia Abu-Jamal's original trial may have been contaminated by the deep-rooted racism that appears to taint the application of the death penalty in Pennsylvania." In late 1999, under a stay of execution, Mumia remained in prison fighting for a new trial.

RACIAL PROFILING

Many black citizens were moved by these dramatic cases of police abuse, and some took to the streets in protest. But unequal police practices also affected ordinary African Americans directly in the form of "racial profiling," or what has been called "Driving While Black" (DWB). These are routine traffic stops by police used as a pretext to search for evidence. This practice is used ostensibly to target drug dealers and is based on the premise that most drug offenses are committed by people of color (mainly blacks and Latinos). Although the premise is factually untrue, the vast majority of motorists routinely stopped as alleged drug carriers are African Americans and Latinos. Between January 1995 and September 1996, the Maryland State Police stopped and searched 823 motorists on Interstate 95, of which 600 were black. Only 19.7 percent of those searched in this corridor were white. Some cases were highly publicized. In 1997 San Diego Chargers football player Shawn Lee and his girlfriend were pulled over, handcuffed, and detained by police for half an hour. The officer claimed that Lee's Jeep Cherokee fit the description of a vehicle stolen earlier that day. Records later revealed that the stolen vehicle was a Honda sedan. In 1998, a Liberian student named Nelson Walker was driving along I-95 in Maryland when he was pulled over by state police for not wearing a seatbelt. The officers proceeded to search his car for illegal drugs, weapons, or other contraband, to the point of dismantling a door panel, a seat panel, and part of the sunroof, but they found nothing. The overwhelming number of incidents like these became evident when victims began to sue and concerned politicians began promoting legislation to outlaw racial profiling. The state of New Jersey alone paid out over $800,000 in out-of-court settlements to victims of racial profiling. Nevertheless, as a result of systematic harassment and surveillance, few African Americans feel safe around the police. Christopher Darden, a black attorney who gained notoriety as a prosecutor in the O.J. Simpson murder case, said that in order to survive routine stops, he had to learn "the rules of the game. . . . Don't move. Don't turn around. Don't give some rookie an excuse to shoot you."

In other words, even those who live on the outskirts of America's crumbling ghettos at times feel like they are living in a police state. Yet, while they have their share of nightmares, of racist humiliation, of invisible barriers, even of violence, they are a little safer, a little more secure, and a lot richer. At moments they are as distant from ghetto residents as white farmers in Iowa. At other times they are as close as kin. In a strange way, the L.A. rebellion simultaneously brought them together and tore them apart. They shared the experience of racial humiliation, of realizing that black life, no matter how much money one has, is valued less than white life. The experience tore them apart because it underscored the growing chasm dividing rich and poor.

AN UNFINISHED STORY

The generation that came of age in the '70s, '80s, and '90s had been called a lot of things: the post-soul generation, the post–civil rights generation, the postindustrial generation. But few standing "at the edge of history," to use the language of the Gary Declaration, thought in terms of being "post" anything. Rather, they entered a new period with tremendous efforts toward racial integration. For others it was the hope for greater political and social control of their lives. For most African Americans it was a combination of both with a little fun and pleasure thrown in for good measure.

Few anticipated the economic, social, and political crises poor urban blacks would have to face, and fewer still imagined the plush black suburbs of Prince Georges County, Maryland, or that several black-owned companies might one day dwarf Motown Records. Although each difficult day questioned their faith in this country, young mothers and fathers hoped that racism would diminish a little and life for their children would be much easier. In some cases their lives *were* much easier; in other cases a racist police officer's bullet or the fists, sticks, and stones of skinheads cut their young lives short.

But this story is not finished yet, and it need not have a tragic ending. The chapters to come will be written by all of us still living, including you who hold this book in your hands. What we add to this story depends, to a large degree, on us . . . all of us: black and white, Latino and Asian, Native American and Arab American, Jew and Gentile, women and men, rich and poor. If there is one thing we have learned from this book, it is that the problems facing African Americans are not simply outgrowths of a crisis in *black* America. They are products of America's crisis. We must constantly remind ourselves that America's future is bound up with the descendants of slaves and the circumstances they must endure. As police brutality victim Rodney King put it in his memorable press conference following the Los Angeles uprising, "We're all stuck here for a while."

Diversity on Trial

ALEXANDER WOHL

In this article, Professor Alexander Wohl explores the legal situation of affirmative action in America. In 1978 the Supreme Court upheld the constitutionality of using race as one factor in the university admissions process, Wohl argues, but it did so with a somewhat ambiguous ruling that is subject to competing interpretations. Recent lower court rulings have been indecisive or even in open conflict with one another, according to Wohl, suggesting that affirmative action may soon head once again to the Supreme Court in search of a decisive ruling. Wohl is an adjunct professor at American University's Washington College of Law.

I f this article had appeared before Tuesday, March 27 [2001], the sentence you are reading now would have said: "A recent decision by a district court judge about admissions policies at the University of Michigan is heartening news for supporters of affirmative action in higher education." Instead, that introductory sentence needs to be replaced with this one: "A recent decision by a district court judge about admissions policies at the University of Michigan is *disheartening* news for supporters of affirmative action in higher education."

What happened?

Actually, as contradictory as those two sentences sound, they're both true. On December 13, 2000, a federal district court judge appointed by Ronald Reagan upheld the constitutionality of race-conscious *undergraduate* admissions at the University of Michigan. Yet a mere three months later, on March 27, another ruling—by another Reagan-appointed judge on the same district court—held that the race-conscious admissions program of the University of Michigan's *law school* is unconstitutional.

These Michigan decisions are only the most recent and overtly contradictory of a panoply of conflicting rulings on affirmative action in higher education that have been handed down by federal courts in the last few years. The Fifth Circuit Court of Appeals in 1996 (ruling on the University of Texas's law school admissions policies, in *Hopwood v. Texas*) and the Ninth Circuit December 4, 2000, (ruling on the University of Washington's law school admissions policies, in *Smith v. University of Washington*), for example, have also made significant—and contrary—decisions about the constitutionality of race-conscious admissions.

The recent rulings in this area reinforce not only how individual judges interpreting the same case law and the same language in the Constitution can reach fundamentally different conclusions, but also how precarious affirmative action policy in higher education has become. The fate of race-conscious admissions policies now likely awaits the decision of a closely divided U.S. Supreme Court.

AN AMBIGUOUS RULING

If—and, as appears increasingly likely, when—the Supreme Court takes up the question of affirmative action in higher education, it won't be the first time it has done so. In 1978, in *Regents of the University of California v. Bakke*, the Supreme Court narrowly, and some would say ambiguously, ruled that race can be considered as one factor in making admissions decisions. Indeed, it is the Court's arguably murky decision in *Bakke*, and in particular Justice Lewis Powell's majority opinion in the case, that have been at the heart of all the recent decisions, both pro–and anti–affirmative action. As the Ninth Circuit recently put it when ruling in favor of race-conscious admissions plans at the University of Washington, "The difficulty with which we are presented is that in *Bakke* none of the other justices fully agreed with Justice Powell's opinion, so we are left with the task of deciding just what the Supreme Court decided."

In his *Bakke* opinion, Justice Powell argued that a diverse student body is a constitutionally permissible goal for a college or university. Race or ethnic background, he wrote, can be a factor in determining a particular candidate's "potential contribution to diversity without the factor of race being decisive." The decisions in favor of race-conscious admissions at the University of Washington's law school and the University of Michigan's undergraduate program drew heavily on Powell's reasoning, and on the conclusion of the majority in *Bakke* that "diversity" is a worthy (and constitutional) goal for institutions of higher education to pursue. In fact, these recent decisions were ringing endorsements of the concept that campus diversity improves the academic environment, an idea most famously supported in the landmark *Brown v. Board of Education* case in 1954.

But the justices produced a plethora of divergent opinions in *Bakke*, with no one opinion commanding a majority in its entirety. Each of six different opinions served to endorse or dissent from portions of what became the Court's opinion, which was the one written by Powell. Powell's primary holding—which struck down the University of California's quota system but upheld the idea of taking race into account in university admissions policies—was joined in part by Justices William Brennan, Byron White, Thurgood Marshall, and Harry Blackmun. Writing separately, concurring in part and dissenting in part, was Justice John Paul Stevens; joining him in dissent were the Court's more conservative members—Chief Justice Warren Burger and Justices Potter Stewart and William Rehnquist.

The confusion about just what the liberal majority of five agreed to has been used ever since by opponents (including the plaintiffs in the recent Washington and Michigan cases) to support the claim that there never was a true majority on the Court in favor of using "diversity" and "academic freedom" to justify the consideration of race in the admissions process.

But while it's true that the liberals on the *Bakke* Court, led by Justice William Brennan, did not join fully in Powell's reasoning, that was because they wanted more, not less, consideration given to race in admissions than Powell's holding advocated. The Ninth Circuit, which upheld the University of Washington's policy, agreed. That court scrutinized the *Bakke* decision and concluded that Justice Brennan and the justices who joined with him did not disagree with Powell's opinion that race can be used as a "plus" factor. "It seems clear," the Ninth Circuit wrote, that in the Supreme Court's majority ruling the justices "saw nothing unconstitutional about a diversity based program that at least purported to take all kinds of special characteristics, and talents, including race, into account." As further evidence of the continuing validity of *Bakke*, the circuit court cited Supreme Court precedent stating that its holdings will be determined by the position taken by the justices who agreed "on the narrowest grounds"; that is, the Ninth Circuit would base its decision on the basic legal principles on which a majority of the Court concurred in *Bakke*.

But exactly what constitutes the "narrowest grounds" has been a major source of contention, not just about *Bakke* specifically but about constitutional interpretation generally. A 1977 ruling, *Marks v. United States* (concerning criminal pornography), identified what the "governing standards" of a court's decision should be when "a fragmented Court decides a case and no single rationale explaining the result enjoys the assent of five Justices." Not surprisingly, how judges apply this aspect of *Marks* to *Bakke* relates to whether or not they believe Justice Powell's opinion spoke for a majority of the Supreme Court on the diversity question.

A LEGAL CHALLENGE

As with virtually all challenges to college admissions programs, both Michigan cases began when white students filed lawsuits against the schools that denied them admission. The students (backed, as they often are in these cases, by the conservative Center for Individual Rights) claimed that by using race as a criterion for admission the schools denied them equal protection of the laws. No one disputes that the schools used race as one factor in those admissions decisions. Nor is there a disagreement about the schools' motivation—to increase diversity. Thus, the question for the courts was whether racial classification, which is—to use the constitutional-law jargon—"inherently suspect," passed the test of "strict scrutiny." In other words, does the university have, as a matter of law, a compelling interest in the attainment of a diverse student body?

Judges who have found schools' admissions programs unconstitutional (including the recent Michigan law school opinion) assert that *Bakke* does not support the idea of educational diversity as a grounds for overcoming the strict-scrutiny test. They also cite a series of Supreme Court rulings on affirmative action in other areas, such as the workplace, which have virtually eliminated the policy in those spheres.

But the judges who upheld the admissions policies of the University of Michigan undergraduate program and of the University of Washington's law school affirmed the constitutionality of pursuing diversity in higher education. Not only did they conclude that this is what a majority in *Bakke* had explicitly held, they also implicitly drew support from the *Brown v. Board of Education* decision, which used social science as a tool for defining constitutional law. Both the Michigan district court and the Ninth Circuit appeals court in Washington ruled that diversity constitutes a compelling governmental interest in the context of higher education that justifies the use of race as one factor in the admissions process. But while the Ninth Circuit used an analysis that pieced together five justices who agreed with Powell on the "narrowest footing," the Michigan judge went even further.

The Michigan court observed the "solid evidence regarding the educational benefits that flow from a racially and ethnically diverse student body" and pointed out the lack of any argument rebutting this evidence. Furthermore, responding to claims about the benefits of the diversity policy being "too amorphous or ill-defined" to pass strict scrutiny, the court said that this argument did not apply in higher education the way it would in, say, the construction industry. Whereas affirmative action in other contexts might aim primarily to remediate past wrongs, "diversity in higher education, by its very nature, is a permanent and ongoing interest."

But the more recent Michigan decision, involving the law school's admissions policy, could hardly have been more different. While acknowledging that racial diversity in the law school population may provide "important and laudable" educational and societal benefits, Judge Bernard A. Friedman concluded that "the attainment of a racially diverse class is not a compelling state interest." In reaching this conclusion, the court appears to have taken almost the opposite position from the earlier Michigan ruling—saying that the only way that affirmative action can be used is as a remedy for past discrimination. While that may currently be the legal standard for affirmative action in the workplace, it has never been held to apply in the educational environment. In rejecting affirmative action in this manner, Judge Friedman allied himself with the 1996 decision in *Hopwood v. Texas* by a panel of the U.S. Circuit Court of Appeals for the Fifth Circuit—an opinion that threw out the University of Texas law school's affirmative action admissions program for African-American and Mexican-American applicants.

The Michigan law school decision is troubling—and dangerous—because it appears to ignore specific questions of evidence. While the court heard weeks of testimony and explicitly acknowledged the importance and legitimacy of diversity as an asset in education, it nonetheless held that these benefits did not present a "compelling interest." The court further closed the door by suggesting that even if racial diversity were a compelling state interest, the school's use of race was not "narrowly tailored" enough to pass constitutional muster. It suggested that the plan was "indistinguishable from a quota system," an approach that a majority in *Bakke* had disallowed.

All these conflicting decisions are rapidly paving the road to the Supreme Court. That's not necessarily good news for advocates of affirmative action. [Then president] Bill Clinton's Justice Department filed briefs in support of the diversity policies in several of the lower-court cases; the Bush administration's attorney general, John Ashcroft, is virtually certain to take the other side. And he'll have formidable assistance in his efforts: The solicitor general–designate, Ted Olson, successfully argued the *Hopwood* case on behalf of the student plaintiffs.

By what avenue is the issue likely to arrive before the Court? And does the Court even want to take on this challenge? It declined to hear Texas's appeal in *Hopwood*. Yet the high court did recently agree to hear arguments in a workplace-related affirmative action case—a possible signal that Court conservatives are feeling confident enough to establish further precedent in this area.

A new Supreme Court precedent could fundamentally redefine affirmative action in higher education, either by clearly denying or clearly reasserting its basic constitutionality. The bottom line—as Justice Brennan used to make clear by simply holding up his hand with all five fingers opened—is who has the votes. It's a principle that the conservative majority on this Court, like the man sitting in the White House as a result of that majority, can readily affirm. While the justices (especially the conservative ones) may talk about *stare decisis*—respect for precedent—their crucial legal decision on affirmative action may come down to ideology.

So how is the Court likely to vote? Two of the current justices were on the high court in 1978 when *Bakke* was decided. The man who wrote the dissent was Justice John Paul Stevens. But Stevens based his 1978 opinion solely on Title VI of the Civil Rights Act—not the Constitution—and concluded that the broader constitutional question of "whether race can ever be used as a factor in an admissions decision is not an issue in this case." What is more, the independent-thinking Stevens, who penned an impassioned dissent in the *Bush v. Gore* decision that put President George W. Bush in the Oval Office, has grown in his appreciation of civil rights law. (It is a measure of how far the Court has moved to the right that the Republican-appointed Stevens, author of the *Bakke* dissent, is today considered to be a member of the so-called liberal bloc of justices.)

Justice William Rehnquist joined Stevens's dissent in *Bakke*.

But unlike Stevens, Rehnquist—now the chief justice—has not budged ideologically since 1978. His conservative philosophy and his other opinions in this area make him an almost certain vote for the elimination of affirmative action. The same goes for Justice Antonin Scalia, a self-proclaimed strict constructionist; he will likely suggest that nowhere in the text of the equal protection clause does it talk about "plus" factors in terms of making decisions about admissions. Justice Anthony Kennedy has also shown great skepticism about affirmative action in previous cases.

Though he is the most obvious beneficiary of affirmative action on the Court, Clarence Thomas has been among the policy's most vociferous opponents. If the anti-diversity justices win a majority in this case, Chief Justice Rehnquist might very well assign authorship of the opinion to the only black justice—the man who replaced Justice Thurgood Marshall, the great civil rights lawyer who argued *Brown*.

On the other side, Justices Ruth Bader Ginsburg, Stephen Breyer, and David Souter would likely hew with Stevens to Justice Powell's protection of a university's rights to include diversity as one factor in the admissions scheme. Thus, in the end, the Supreme Court's decision—and the future of affirmative action—may depend on the opinion of a single jurist who regularly casts the swing vote on this Court: Justice Sandra Day O'Connor.

THE O'CONNOR FACTOR

In this area of the law, O'Connor has been typically judicious and limited in her approach. On one occasion, she voted to strike down preferences in layoffs of more senior white employees when no evidence of previous discrimination against the black employees was present. But on another occasion, she voted to uphold a voluntary affirmative action plan for women when there was a wide disparity in the numbers of men and women in the top ranks. It's possible to imagine O'Connor using a new case to construct a rationale either for or against diversity.

One likely option O'Connor will consider is to predicate her decision on the unique role of education and university admissions in our society, as distinct from its systems of hiring and firing. To this end, a concurring opinion in *Hopwood* by Judge Jacques L. Wiener, Jr., of the Fifth Circuit may prove prescient. In disagreeing with the appeals court's conclusion that diversity can never be a compelling governmental interest in a public graduate school, Weiner cited Justice O'Connor's opinion in *Adarand Constructors, Inc. v. Pena*, the case that largely helped do away with affirmative action in the employment context. Justice O'Connor's opinion in that case, Judge Weiner noted, "expressly states that *Adarand* is not the death knell of affirmative action—to which I would add, especially not in the framework of achieving diversity in public graduate schools."

One final point to consider is that O'Connor has taken on Powell's role as the Court's swing vote; for that reason, she often strives to provide a decision limited in scope. The diversity policy expressed in Powell's *Bakke* opinion represents the embodiment of that philosophy: It's a limited—not a sweeping—rationale for affirmative action in higher education. O'Connor therefore might vote to uphold it.

The immediate implications of a Supreme Court ruling are enormous. When the University of Texas law school eliminated race as a plus factor after *Hopwood*, the percentage of the entering class that was African American dropped from 5.8 percent (29 students) to 0.9 percent (four students). Similar declines in law school enrollments by racial minorities occurred in California following the passage of Proposition 209, which eliminated affirmative action in the state's university system.

But this judicial decision—like the policy under consideration itself—should be about more than just numbers. If the Supreme Court upholds the constitutionality of affirmative action programs, it will reinforce America's commitment not just to diversity but to the idea that the nation must continue to take extra steps to build an inclusive society and repair the effects of a long history of discrimination, particularly in an area as crucial for the long term as education.

The Debt

RANDALL ROBINSON

In this piece, Randall Robinson—the founder and president of
TransAfrica, an international human rights organization—explores
the issue of whether black Americans deserve to be compensated
for two and a half centuries of slavery. In his view the answer is
clearly yes, and he argues that the money that slaves should have been
paid for their labor is money that is owing. As Robinson sees it, slavery had a terrible effect not only on those who were slaves, but on
generations of their descendants, and he illustrates this by tracing his
view of the emergence of a typical contemporary black male. Justice, he argues, is long overdue.

On January 5, 1993, Congressman John Conyers, a black
Democrat from Detroit, introduced in Congress a bill to
"acknowledge the fundamental injustice, cruelty, brutality, and
inhumanity of slavery in the United States and the 13 American colonies between 1619 and 1865 and to establish a commission to examine the institution of slavery, subsequent *de jure*
and *de facto* racial and economic discrimination against African
Americans, and the impact of these forces on living African
Americans, to make recommendations to the Congress on appropriate remedies, and for other purposes."

The bill, which did not ask for reparations for the descendants of slaves but merely a commission to study the effects of
slavery, won from the 435-member U.S. House of Representatives only 28 cosponsors, 18 of whom were black.

The measure was referred to the House Committee on the
Judiciary and from there to the House Subcommittee on Civil
and Constitutional Rights. The bill has never made it out of
committee.

More than twenty years ago, black activist James Foreman interrupted the Sunday morning worship service of the largely white Riverside Church in New York City and read a *Black Manifesto* which called upon American churches and synagogues to pay $500 million as "a beginning of the reparations due us as people who have been exploited and degraded, brutalized, killed and persecuted." Foreman followed by promising to penalize poor response with disruptions of the churches' program agency operations. Though Foreman's tactics were broadly criticized in the mainstream press, the issue of reparations itself elicited almost no thoughtful response. This had been the case by then for nearly a century, during which divergent strains of black thought had offered a variety of reparation proposals. The American white community had turned a deaf ear almost uniformly.

Gunnar Myrdal, a widely respected thinker, wrote of dividing up plantations into small parcels for sale to ex-slaves on long-term installment plans. He theorized that American society's failure to secure ex-slaves with an agrarian economic base had led ultimately to an entrenched segregated society, a racial cast system. But while Myrdal had seen white landowners being compensated for their land, he never once proposed recompense of any kind for the ex-slave he saw as in need of an economic base. In fact, in his book on the subject, *An American Dilemma,* Myrdal never once uses the words: reparation, restitution, indemnity, or compensation.

In the early 1970s Boris Bittker, a Yale Law School professor, wrote a book, *The Case for Black Reparations,* which made the argument that slavery, Jim Crow, and a general climate of race-based discrimination in America had combined to do grievous social and economic injury to African Americans. He further argued that sustained government-sponsored violations had rendered distinctions between *de jure* and *de facto* segregation meaningless for all practical purposes. Damages, in his view, were indicated in the form of an allocation of resources to some program that could be crafted for black reparations. The book evoked little in the way of scholarly response or follow-up.

The slim volume was sent to me by an old friend who once worked for me at TransAfrica, Ibrahim Gassama, now a law professor at the University of Oregon. I had called Ibrahim in Eugene to talk over the legal landscape for crafting arguments for a claim upon the federal and state governments for restitution or reparations to the derivative victims of slavery and the racial abuse that followed in its wake.

"It's the strangest thing," Ibrahim had said to me. "We law professors talk about every imaginable subject, but when the issue of reparations is raised among white professors, many of whom are otherwise liberal, it is met with silence. Clearly, there is a case to be made for this as an unpaid debt. Our claim may not be enforceable in the courts because the federal government has to agree to allow itself to be sued. In fact, this will probably have to come out of the Congress as other American reparations have. Nonetheless, there is clearly a strong case to be made. But, I tell you, the mere raising of the subject produces a deathly silence, not unlike the silence that greeted the book I'm sending you."

Derrick Bell, who was teaching at Harvard Law School while I was a student there in the late 1960s, concluded his review of Bittker's book in a way that may explain the reaction Ibrahim got from his colleagues:

> Short of a revolution, the likelihood that blacks today will obtain direct payments in compensation for their subjugation as slaves before the Emancipation Proclamation, and their exploitation as quasi-citizens since, is no better than it was in 1866, when Thaddeus Stevens recognized that his bright hope of "forty acres and a mule" for every freedman had vanished "like the baseless fabric of a vision."

THE ECONOMIC GAP

If Bell is right that African Americans will not be compensated for the massive wrongs and social injuries inflicted upon them by their government, during and after slavery, then there is *no* chance that America can solve its racial problems—if solving these problems means, as I believe it must, closing the yawning economic gap between blacks and whites in this country. The gap was opened by the 246-year practice of slavery. It has been resolutely nurtured since in law and public behavior. It has now ossified. It is structural. Its framing beams are disguised only by the counterfeit manners of a hypocritical governing class.

For twelve years Nazi Germany inflicted horrors upon European Jews. And Germany paid. It paid Jews individually. It paid the state of Israel. For two and a half centuries, Europe and America inflicted unimaginable horrors upon Africa and its people. Europe not only paid nothing to Africa in compensation, but followed the slave trade with the remapping of Africa for further European economic exploitation. (European governments have yet even to accede to Africa's request for the return of Africa's art treasures looted along with its natural resources during the century-long colonial era.)

While President Lincoln supported a plan during the Civil War to compensate slave owners for their loss of "property," his successor, Andrew Johnson, vetoed legislation that would have provided compensation to ex-slaves.

Under the Southern Homestead Act, ex-slaves were given six months to purchase land at reasonably low rates without competition from white southerners and northern investors. But, owing to their destitution, few ex-slaves were able to take advantage of the homesteading program. The largest number that did were concentrated in Florida, numbering little more than three thousand. The soil was generally poor and unsuitable for farming purposes. In any case, the ex-slaves had no money on which to subsist for months while waiting for crops, or the scantest wherewithal to purchase the most elementary farming implements. The program failed. In sum, the United States government provided no compensation to the victims of slavery.

THE NEED TO FIGHT FOR REPARATIONS

Perhaps I should say a bit here about why the question of reparations is critical to finding a solution to our race problems.

This question—and how blacks gather to pose it—is a good measure of our psychological readiness as a community to pull ourselves abreast here at home and around the world. I say this because no outside community can be more interested in solving our problems than we. Derrick Bell suggested in his review of Bittker's book that the white power structure would never support reparations because to do so would operate against its interests. I believe Bell is right in that view. The initiative must come from blacks, broadly, widely, implacably.

But what exactly will black enthusiasm, or lack thereof, measure? There is no linear solution to any of our problems, for our problems are not merely technical in nature. By now, after 380 years of unrelenting psychological abuse, the biggest part of our problem is inside us: in how we have come to see ourselves, in our damaged capacity to validate a course for ourselves without outside approval.

The issue here is not whether or not we can, or will, win reparations. The issue rather is whether we will fight for reparations, because we have decided for ourselves that they are our due. In 1915, into the sharp teeth of southern Jim Crow hostility, Cornelius J. Jones filed a lawsuit against the United States Department of the Treasury in an attempt to recover sixty-eight million dollars for former slaves. He argued that, through a federal tax placed on raw cotton, the federal government had benefited financially from the sale of cotton that slave labor had produced, and for which the black men, women, and children who had produced the cotton had not been paid. Jones's was a straightforward proposition. The monetary value of slaves' labor, which he estimated to be sixty-eight million dollars, had been appropriated by the United States government. A debt existed. It had to be paid to the, by then, ex-slaves or their heirs.

Where was the money?

A federal appeals court held that the United States could not be sued without its consent and dismissed the so-called Cotton Tax case. But the court never addressed Cornelius J. Jones's question about the federal government's appropriation of property—the labor of blacks who had worked the cotton fields—that had never been compensated.

Let me try to drive the point home here: through keloids of suffering, through coarse veils of damaged self-belief, lost direction, misplaced compass, shit-faced resignation, racial transmutation, black people worked long, hard, killing days, years, centuries—and they were never *paid*. The value of their labor went into others' pockets—plantation owners, northern entrepreneurs, state treasuries, the United States government.

Where was the money?

Where *is* the money?

There is a debt here.

I know of no statute of limitations either legally or morally that would extinguish it. Financial quantities are nearly as indestructible as matter. Take away here, add there, interest compounding annually, over the years, over the whole of the twentieth century.

Where is the money?

Jews have asked this question of countries and banks and corporations and collectors and any who had been discovered at the end of the slimy line holding in secret places the gold, the art, the money that was the rightful property of European Jews before the Nazi terror. Jews have demanded what was their due and received a fair measure of it.

Clearly, how blacks respond to the challenge surrounding the simple demand for restitution will say a lot more about us *and do a lot more for us* than the demand itself would suggest. We would show ourselves to be responding as any normal people would to victimization were we to assert collectively in our demands for restitution that, for 246 years and with the complicity of the United States government, hundreds of millions of black people endured unimaginable cruelties—kidnapping, sale as livestock, deaths in the millions during terror-filled sea voyages, backbreaking toil, beatings, rapes, castrations, maimings, murders. We would begin a healing of our psyches were the most public case made that whole peoples lost religions, languages, customs, histories, cultures, children, mothers, fathers. It would make us more forgiving of ourselves, more self-approving, more self-understanding to see, *really see,* that on three continents and a string of islands, survivors had little choice but to piece together whole new cultures from the rubble shards of what theirs had once been. And they were never made whole. And never compensated. Not one red cent.

Left behind to gasp for self-regard in the vicious psychological wake of slavery are history's orphans played by the brave black shells of their ancient forebears, people so badly damaged that they cannot *see* the damage, or how their government may have been partly, if not largely, responsible for the disabling injury that by now has come to seem normal and unattributable.

Until America's white ruling class accepts the fact that the book never closes on massive unredressed social wrongs, America can have no future as one people. Questions must be raised, to American private, as well as, public institutions. Which American families and institutions, for instance, were endowed in perpetuity by the commerce of slavery? And how do we square things with slavery's modern victims from whom all natural endowments were stolen? What is a fair measure of restitution for this, the most important of all American human rights abuses?

If one leaves aside the question of punitive damages to do a rough reckoning of what might be fair in basic compensation, we might look first at the status of today's black male.

An Example

For purposes of illustration, let us picture one representative individual whose dead-end crisis in contemporary America symbolizes the plight of millions. At various times in his life he will likely be in jail or unemployed or badly educated or sick from a curable ailment or dead from violence.

What happened to him? From what did he emerge?

His great-great-grandfather was born a slave and died a slave. Great-great-grandfather's labors enriched not only his white southern owner but also shipbuilders, sailors, ropemakers, caulkers, and countless other northern businesses that serviced and benefited from the cotton trade built upon slavery. Great-great-grandfather had only briefly known his mother and father before being sold off from them to a plantation miles away. He had no idea where in Africa his people had originally come from, what language they had spoken or customs they had practiced. Although certain Africanisms—falsetto singing, the ring shout, and words like *yam*—had survived, he did not know that their origins were African.

He was of course compulsorily illiterate. His days were trials of backbreaking work and physical abuse with no promise of relief. He had no past and no future. He scratched along only because some biological instinct impelled him to survive.

His son, today's black male's great-grandfather, was also born into slavery and, like his father, wrenched so early from his parents that he could scarcely remember them. At the end of the Civil War, he was nineteen years old. While he was pleased to no longer be a slave, he was uncertain that the new status would yield anything in real terms that was very much different from the life (if you could call it that) that he had been living. He too was illiterate and completely without skills.

He was one of four million former slaves wandering rootlessly around in the defeated South. He trusted no whites, whether from the North or South. He had heard during the war that even President Lincoln had been urging blacks upon emancipation to leave the United States en masse for colonies that would be set up in Haiti and Liberia. In fact, Lincoln had invited a group of free blacks to the White House in August 1862 and told them: "Your race suffers greatly, many of them, by living among us, while ours suffer from your presence. In a word we suffer on each side. If this is admitted, it affords a reason why we should be separated."

Today's black male's great-grandfather knew nothing of Haiti or Liberia, although he had a good idea why Lincoln wanted to ship blacks to such places. By 1866 his life had remained a trial of instability and rootlessness. He had no money and little more than pickup work. He and other blacks in the

South were faced as well with new laws that were not unlike the antebellum Slave Codes. The new measures were called Black Codes and, as John Hope Franklin noted in *From Slavery to Freedom,* they all but guaranteed that

> the control of blacks by white employers was about as great as that which slaveholders had exercised. Blacks who quit their job could be arrested and imprisoned for breach of contract. They were not allowed to testify in court except in cases involving members of their own race. Numerous fines were imposed for seditious speeches, insulting gestures or acts, absence from work, violating curfew, and the possession of firearms. There was, of course, no enfranchisement of blacks and no indication that in the future they could look forward to full citizenship and participation in a democracy.

Although some blacks received land in the South under the Southern Homestead Act of 1866, the impression that every ex-slave would receive "forty acres and a mule" as a gift of the government never became a reality. Great-grandfather, like the vast majority of the four million former slaves, received nothing and died penniless in 1902—but not before producing a son who was born in 1890 and later became the first of his line to learn to read.

THE PERSISTENCE OF SLAVERY

Two decades into the new century, having inherited nothing in the way of bootstraps with which to hoist himself, and faced with unremitting racial discrimination, Grandfather became a sharecropper on land leased from whites whose grandparents had owned at least one of his forebears. The year was 1925 and neither Grandfather nor his wife was allowed to vote. His son would join him in the cotton fields under the broiling sun of the early 1930s. They worked twelve hours or more a day and barely eked out a living. Grandfather had managed to finish the fifth grade before leaving school to work full time. Inasmuch as he talked like the people he knew, and like his parents and their parents before them, his syntax and pronunciation bore the mark of the unlettered. Grandfather wanted badly that his son's life not mirror his, but was failing depressingly in producing for the boy any better opportunity than that with which he himself had been presented. Not only had he no money, but he survived against the punishing strictures of southern segregation that allowed for blacks the barest leavings in education, wages, and political freedom. He was trapped and afraid to raise his voice against a system that in many respects resembled slavery, now a mere seventy years gone.

Grandfather drank and expressed his rage in beatings administered to his wife and his son. In the early 1940s Grandfather disappeared into a deep depression and never seemed the same again.

Grandfather's son, the father of today's black male, periodically attended segregated schools, first in a rural area near the family's leased cotton patch and later in a medium-sized segregated southern city. He learned to read passably but never finished high school. He was not stigmatized for this particular failure because the failure was not exceptional in the only world that he had ever known.

Ingrained low expectation, when consciously faced, invites impenetrable gloom. Thus, Father did not dwell on the meagerness of his life chances. Any penchant he may have had for introspection, like his father before him, he drowned in corn spirits on Friday nights. He was a middle-aged laborer and had never been on first-name terms with anyone who was not a laborer like himself. He worked for whites and, as far as he could tell, everyone in his family before him had. Whites had, to him, the best of everything—houses, cars, schools, movie theaters, neighborhoods. Black neighborhoods he could tell from simply looking at them, even before he saw the people. And it was not just that the neighborhoods were poor. No, he had subconsciously likened something inside himself, a jagged rent in his ageless black soul, to the sagging wooden tenement porches laden with old household objects—ladders, empty flowerpots, wagons—that rested on them, often wrong side up, for months at a time. The neighborhoods, lacking sidewalks, streetlights, and sewage systems, had, like Father and other blacks, preserved themselves by not caring. Hunkered down. Gone inside themselves, turning blank, sullen faces to the outside world.

The world hadn't bothered to notice.

Father died of heart disease at the age of forty-five just before the Voting Rights Act was passed in 1965. Like his ancestors who had lived and died in slavery in centuries before, he was never allowed to cast a vote in his life. Little else distinguished his life from theirs, save a subsistence wage, the freedom to walk around in certain public areas, and the ability to read a newspaper, albeit slowly.

Parallel lines never touch, no matter how far in time and space they extend.

TODAY'S BLACK MALE

They had been declared free—four million of them. Some had simply walked off plantations during the war in search of Union forces. Others had become brazenly outspoken to their white masters toward the war's conclusion. Some had remained loyal to their masters to the end. Abandoned, penniless and unskilled, to the mercies of a humiliated and hostile South, millions of men, women, and children trudged into the false freedom of the Jim Crow South with virtually nothing in the way of recompense, preparation, or even national apology.

It is from this condition that today's black male emerged.

His social crisis is so alarming that the United States Commission on Civil Rights by the spring of 1999 had made it the subject of an unusual two-day conference. "This is a very real and serious and difficult issue," said Mary Frances Berry, chair of the commission. "This crisis has broad implications for the future of the race."

The black male is far more likely than his white counterpart to be in prison, to be murdered, to have no job, to fail in school, to become seriously ill. His life will be shorter by seven years, his chances of finishing high school smaller—74 percent as opposed to 86 percent for his white counterpart. Exacerbating an already crushing legacy of slavery-based social disabilities, he faces fresh discrimination daily in modern America. In the courts of ten states and the District of Columbia, he is ten times more likely to be imprisoned than his white male counterpart for the same offense. If convicted on a drug charge, he will likely serve a year more in prison than his white male counterpart will for the same charge. While he and his fellow black males constitute 15 percent of the nation's drug users, they make up 33 percent of those arrested for drug use and 57 percent of those convicted. And then they die sooner, and at higher rates of chronic illnesses like AIDS, hypertension, diabetes, cancer, stroke, and Father's killer, heart disease.

Saddest of all, they have no clear understanding of why such debilitating fates have befallen them. There were no clues in their public school education. No guideposts in the popular culture. Theirs was the "now" culture. They felt no impulse to look behind for causes.

CHAPTER 6

PERSONAL NARRATIVES

AMERICAN
SOCIAL
MOVEMENTS

I'll Know Victory
or Defeat

JAMES H. MEREDITH

James H. Meredith was the first black person to attend the University of Mississippi and was able to do so only under the protection of federal troops sent by U.S. Attorney General Robert Kennedy. In this article, written shortly after he began attending Ole Miss in the fall of 1962, Meredith talks about the riots on campus, his first few weeks of class, and his feelings and experiences as the first and only black student there. Meredith successfully graduated in 1964, and in June 1966 started a solitary "March Against Fear" from Memphis, Tennessee, to Jackson, Mississippi. Although he was struck down by a sniper's bullet, he managed to survive and was later able to resume the march.

I f you asked me when it all began—what brought me to the campus in Oxford that first week in October—I guess I would say it began when I was a boy in Kosciusko, up in the hill country of Mississippi, where I was born. I used to lie in bed and dream about a city—I didn't know what city or where it was—I just knew it would be different from Kosciusko, because I didn't like the way things were there.

Kosciusko isn't altogether typical of Mississippi, I would say. It is an area of small farms, and most of the farmers, Negro and white, own their own places. I think the Negroes there might be a little more progressive than in some other parts of the state. Some Negroes there—my father, for example—have been voting for as long as I know of. I think you'll find that many progressive Negroes come from an area like this, where they own their own land. Still, I certainly can't say I liked it in

Kosciusko. They tell me I was always strong on the race issue when I was young. For example, I remember a wealthy white man who used to go around town handing out nickels and dimes to Negro children. I never would take any.

In Kosciusko I grew up between things. Part of my family was much older than I was, and part was much younger. It was like being an only child. I really only got to know my brothers and sisters later. Also, I lived in the same country and went to school in town. In small towns in the South you're either a "city boy" or a "country boy," but I wasn't either. I got used to taking care of things by myself.

When I was 16 I left Kosciusko to finish my last year of high school in St. Petersburg, Florida. I had a desire to go to a better school, and I had an uncle and a sister living there. I graduated from high school in June of 1951 and enlisted in the Air Force the next month. I had a brother in the Air Force, but that wasn't the reason I joined. It was common knowledge among Negroes that the Air Force was a better branch of service for them.

INFLUENCE OF AIR FORCE DUTY

Certainly my Air Force days were the most influential time of my life. I served in nothing but integrated units. It seems to me the integration of the armed forces is one of the most important things that has happened to the Negro in the United States. For that reason, I thought it was particularly unfortunate that the Army apparently resegregated its units in Oxford after the night of campus rioting. If Negroes could fight side by side with whites around the world, they should be able to serve with them in Mississippi.

I never had any "bad" incidents when I was in the Air Force. There were occasional small things, reminders that a Negro was a Negro. I remember when I was in basic training at Sampson Air Force Base in New York State, all of us were invited to spend weekends with families in Syracuse. I spent a weekend with a white family there, and they were very nice, but they kept reminding me in subtle ways that they were being unusually nice—in other words, they didn't have to do this; it was just a favor. There is always that air of difference about being a Negro that you can never quite touch.

But life was pretty good in the Air Force. As I say, I served in nothing but integrated units, and everything was OK as far as promotions went too. I remember very well one particular hearing for promotion, when I was up for staff sergeant. I was to go before a board of three colonels. Usually they question you about your qualifications and try to decide whether or not you can take on the responsibilities of the next rank. I came up before the board just two months after the Supreme Court school-desegregation decision in 1954, and they didn't ask me anything about my qualifications. All they asked about was my opinion of the decision, what my family thought about it, and all that. Well, I told them. I'll always remember that when it was over and I had made staff sergeant, they told me they were with me in the struggle but that "the outcome will depend on you." I took that "you" to mean Negroes, all Negroes, and I guess it has been sort of a badge of responsibility ever since.

ACCEPTED ABROAD

In 1955 I reenlisted. I always had it in mind to come back to Mississippi and study law, but I didn't think I was ready then for the responsibilities I would have to face, so I reenlisted. I was in Japan from 1957 till 1960, and there isn't any doubt that this was the settling-down point for me. I decided not only what I wanted to do, which I have known for a long time in a vague way, but how to go about doing it.

Being in Japan was an amazing experience. Negroes say, "When you're in Japan you have to look in a mirror to remember you're a Negro," and it's true. Japan is the only place where I have not felt the "air of difference."

I was surprised that the Japanese people were so aware of the racial situation in America. For instance, I met a boy—I don't suppose he was more than 12 or 13—and he knew more about Little Rock than most American kids that age. He was amazed when I told him I was from Mississippi and that I intended to go back. This kind of reaction further convinced me that I would go back to Mississippi and try to improve these conditions. I was discharged in July 1960, and by the end of the month I was back in Kosciusko.

I entered Jackson State College, a Negro school in Jackson, and quickly met other students who felt as I did—that Negroes in Mississippi did not have the rights of full citizens, including the right to the best education the state offered. Someone had to seek admission to the University of Mississippi, and I decided to do it. But there were many of us involved. Although the lawsuit was mine, the others were with me, and I sought their advice on every move I made.

As soon as I filed application for admission, I contacted Medgar Evers, Mississippi field secretary for the N.A.A.C.P. [The National Association for the Advancement of Colored People], and through him I asked for N.A.A.C.P. legal aid. Mrs. Constance Motley, associate counsel of the N.A.A.C.P. Legal Defense Fund, came to my assistance. The N.A.A.C.P. was prompt and efficient, and that was of prime importance. There was a great morale factor here, and every time we called them, they were there.

The court fight was long, and there were times when I wondered if it would be successful. I kept winning in court, but I didn't get any nearer to the university. Finally, after the Fifth Circuit Court of Appeals had said I should be registered, I felt the responsibility was the Federal Government's; it was out of my hands to do anything.

DECIDING TO ACT

People have asked me if I wasn't terribly afraid the night we went to Oxford. No, my apprehensions came a long time before that. The hardest thing in human nature is to decide to act. I was doing all right in the Air Force. I got married in 1956, and my wife was able to work as a civil servant on the same bases where I was stationed. I had to give this up, this established way of things, this status, and try something new and unknown. That's where the big decision was—not here, last month, but there, a couple of years ago. Once I made that decision, things just had to happen the way they happened.

I think maybe a quote from Theodore Roosevelt that I read somewhere was more important than anything else in helping me make this decision. I think I read it around 1952, and I clipped it out, and everywhere I've gone since then—every place I've lived or everywhere I've worked—I have put that saying in front of me. I guess I must have read it two or three thousand times by now. It says, "It is not the critic who counts. ... The credit belongs to the man who is actually in the arena, whose face is marred by dust and sweat and blood ... who at the best knows in the end the triumph of high achievement, and who at the worst, if he fails, at least fails while daring greatly, so that his place will never be with those cold and timid souls who know neither victory nor defeat." At different times different parts of that quotation have been important to me, but when I made the decision to return to Mississippi and later to enroll at the university, the part I kept seeing was the part about "cold and timid souls who know neither victory nor defeat." I didn't want to be one of those.

FEAR IS JUST ANOTHER OBSTACLE

As far as fear of death or personal injury goes—and I consider this most important for everybody to understand—I put death or the fear of getting hurt in the same category with legal objections to my entering the university, or moral objections, or objections on grounds of custom. They are all on the same level. They are all just ways to keep me out of the university, and no one is any more important than any other. It wouldn't matter if I stumbled and fell and couldn't go to classes or whether I cut my finger and couldn't write for a month or whether I was shot and killed—they're all just things in my way. I might do quite a bit to put a stop to the act of being killed. I have done this several times already—I've taken the advice of the Federal marshals on several occasions, for instance. But this was because, if something happened to me, it would have put everything back as far as the Negroes in Mississippi are concerned. If I have lost an hour's sleep in recent weeks, it has been over some philosophical point, or through apprehension or not succeeding in entering the university, and of discouraging others from trying if I failed, but not over what might happen to me personally.

I was sure that if I were harmed or killed, somebody else would take my place one day. I would hate to think another Negro would have to go through that ordeal, but I would hate worse to think there wouldn't be another who would do it.

I had an older brother who was scary as a boy. Back home he wouldn't go certain places after dark or walk here or there. I always walked wherever I wanted. I walked four miles to Scout meetings at night, and I always went through all the hollows and the places where you were supposed to be afraid to go. I must admit my hair has stood up on my head at times, but I never ran. They used to say, "If you see a 'hant' put your hand on it." Most of the time you find it isn't there. I think it's an utter waste of time to worry about dying. It's living that matters—doing something to justify being here on God's green earth. I do what I do because I must. I've never felt I had a choice. There is some urge that I can't explain easily—I guess that's as close as I can come to defining it.

A Chance to Develop

There is something else here, too, and it's hard to say right. People can misunderstand it. But it's this—generally at home I was always thought to be pretty smart. I wasn't particularly proud of it; it was just almost a fact of life. There was an expectation or a more or less acknowledged fact that I was one of the sharpest in the group. I was a champion in my group in Mississippi, but then, when I went to Florida to change high schools, I wasn't a champion at all. I had to fight to keep up. I hadn't been prepared. Since then, one of the biggest things in my life is that I have always felt I was never able to develop my talents. I have felt many times that, given the opportunity, I could develop into practically anything. Many times I have been angry at the world for not giving me an opportunity to develop. I am sure this has been a strong motivating force with me, and I'm sure it is with many Negroes. Since then I've always tried to see myself in relation to the whole society. Too many Negroes see themselves only in relation to other Negroes. But that's not good enough. We have to see ourselves in the whole society. If America isn't for everybody, it isn't America.

Through all that has happened I have tried to remain detached and objective. I have had all sorts of reactions to things that have happened, but mostly they have been personal reactions and realistic reactions, both at the same time. When I was in the middle of the force of marshals being gathered to take me to Oxford I thought, personally, how utterly ridiculous this was, what a terrible waste of time and money and energy, to iron out some rough spots in our civilization. But realistically I knew that these changes were necessary. I knew change was a threat to people and that they would fight it and that this was the only way it could be accomplished.

PAIN AND FEAR

I have tried to be detached and realistic. When we were turned away the first time I tried to register at the university, and especially the second time, at the State Capitol in Jackson, I saw the mobs and heard them jeering, "Go home, nigger" and that stuff, but I never recognized them as individuals at all, even those who showed the greatest contempt for me. I felt they were not personally attacking me but that they were protesting a change and this was something they felt they must do. I thought it was impersonal. Some of them were crying, and their crying indicated to me even more the pain of change and the fear of things they did not know. I feel the people were keyed up by the actions of their leaders. With Gov. Ross Barnett taking the position he did, the people were bound to act that way, and it didn't really have anything to do with me personally. That's the way I saw it.

I might add that I thought the governor put on a pretty

good performance. The first time, when he turned us away at the university, he reminded me of Charlton Heston, I believe it was, in a movie about Andrew Jackson. Very dramatic.

I don't think I have had a real low point in recent weeks. It always seemed to me it was the Government's job to carry out the court order and it would be done. The most annoying time was when there was so much talk about a possible deal between the Federal Government and Governor Barnett. But when the Federal officers told me we were going that Sunday, just a few minutes before we took off for Oxford, the annoyance disappeared.

ARRIVING ON CAMPUS

When we landed in Oxford it was almost dark. We got in a car and I remember seeing a truckload of marshals in front of us and one behind. I went straight to the university and was taken to my rooms—an apartment, I guess you could call it. Since they knew some Government men would be staying with me, I had two bedrooms and a living room and a bathroom. The first thing I did was make my bed. When the trouble started, I couldn't see or hear very much of it. Most of it was at the other end of the campus, and besides I didn't look out the window. I think I read a newspaper and went to bed around 10 o'clock. I was awakened several times in the night by the noise and shooting outside, but it wasn't near me, and I had no way of knowing what was going on. Some of the students in my dormitory banged their doors for a while and threw some bottles in the halls, but I slept pretty well all night.

I woke up about six-thirty in the morning and looked out and saw the troops. There was a slight smell of tear gas in my room, but I still didn't know what had gone on during the night, and I didn't find out until some marshals came and told me how many people were hurt and killed. I had gotten to know these marshals pretty well in recent weeks, and I was so sorry about this. Some supposedly responsible newspapermen asked me if I thought attending the university was worth all this death and destruction. That really annoyed me. Of course

I was sorry! I didn't want that sort of thing. I believe it could have been prevented by responsible political leaders. I understand the President and the attorney general were up most of the night. They had all the intelligence at their disposal, and I believe they handled it to the best of their knowledge and ability. I think it would have been much worse if we had waited any longer. Social change is a painful thing, but it depends on the people at the top. Here they were totally opposed—the state against the Federal Government. There was bound to be trouble, and there was trouble.

Monday morning at eight o'clock I registered, and at nine I went to a class in Colonial American History. I was a few minutes late, and I took a seat at the back of the room. The professor was lecturing on the background in England, conditions there at the time of the colonization of America, and he paid no special attention when I entered. I think there were about a dozen students in the class. One said hello to me, and the others were silent. I remember a girl—the only girl there, I think—and she was crying, but it might have been from the tear gas in the room. I was crying from it myself.

I had three classes scheduled that day. I went to two, and the third didn't meet because there was too much gas in the room. No marshals were in the classrooms with me, nor were they all week.

SWAMPED WITH MAIL

I have received hundreds of telegrams and more than 1,000 letters, most of them expressions of support. One guy sent me a piece of singed rope, and another sent a poem, I guess you'd have to call it:

> *Roses are red. Violets are blue:*
> *I've killed one nigger and might as well make it two.*

But most or the letters and telegrams have supported me, and some of them have been really touching—letters from 10- and 11-year-olds who think I'm right and offer me their help and that sort of thing.

As far as my relations with the students go, I make it a practice to be courteous. I don't force myself on them, but that's not my nature anyway. Many or them—most, I'd say—have been courteous, and the faculty members certainly have been. When I hear the jeers and the catcalls "We'll get you, nigger" and all that—I don't consider it personal. I get the idea people are just having a little fun. I think it's tragic that they have to have this kind of fun about me, but many of them are children of the men who lead Mississippi today, and I wouldn't expect them to act any other way. They have to act the way they do. I think I understand human nature enough to understand that.

It hasn't been all bad. Many students have spoken to me very pleasantly. They have stopped banging doors and throwing bottles into my dormitory now.

One day a fellow from my hometown sat down at my table in the cafeteria. "If you're here to get an education, I'm for you," he said. "If you're here to cause trouble, I'm against you." That seemed fair enough to me.

MARSHALS ARE A DISTRACTION

I am taking five courses—Colonial American History; a political science course called American Political Parties, Theories and Pressure Groups; French literature; English literature; and algebra. I expect to be able to get my B.A. in history, with a minor in political science, in two semesters and one summer, if everything goes right.

I'm not sure what I will do in the future. A lot depends on how things go at the university. We are just at the beginning of a process of change in Mississippi. I would like to help that process along, and that probably would mean some kind of job in public life. Whether this will be possible in Mississippi or not we'll just have to wait to see. I do know this: If I can't live in Mississippi, I very definitely will leave the country.

If the decision is made to keep the marshals and troops on the campus until I complete my course, it is all right with me, but certainly I hope that won't be necessary. I think the marshals have been superb. They have had an image of America—that the law must be obeyed, no matter what they may think of it or what anybody else may think of it—but they are certainly a distraction on the campus. The thing that grieves me most about all this is that the students are not getting the best college results because they're spending too much time looking on at these various events involving me. I didn't get much studying done that first week, and I don't think anybody else did.

Personally the year will be a hardship for me. My wife will be in college in Jackson. Our son John Howard, who will be three in January, is living with my parents in Kosciusko. I expect to see them both very often, but I don't think families should live apart. On the other hand, this is nothing new to my wife. We spent most of our courtship discussing my plan to come back to Mississippi some day, and I guess you could say her understanding that I would try to do this sometime was almost part of the marriage contract. She has been truly marvelous through all of it. I called her three nights after the trouble, and she picked up the phone and was so calm you'd have thought we just finished a game of 500 rummy and she won. She's a remarkable woman.

I don't think this has had any effect on my family in Kosciusko. I have talked to my father. He asks me how I am, and I ask him how he is. He knows what I mean by the question, and I know what he means by the answer. That's the way it is in our family.

I don't pretend that all the problems are over. But, whatever the problems are, I don't expect them to be too much for me. Nobody really knows where his breaking point is, and I can't say I know where mine is. But I know one thing—in the past the Negro has not been allowed to receive the education he needs. If this is the way it must be accomplished, and I believe it is, then it is not too high a price to pay.

I've Been to the Mountaintop

MARTIN LUTHER KING JR.

In early April 1963, Martin Luther King Jr. was in Memphis, Tennessee, to support striking sanitation workers. In this speech, delivered at Bishop Charles Mason Temple on April 3, he expresses his gratitude for having lived in the second half of the twentieth century, a period witnessing what he calls "the human rights revolution." He also discusses his own involvement in the civil rights movement and how he and others overcame being attacked by police dogs and water cannons. At the close of his address, King recalls the story of his being stabbed several years earlier by a demented person, and again says that he is grateful he lived and was able to continue his involvement in the civil rights movement. King concludes by noting that there are difficult days ahead and increasing threats of violence against him, but he says that he is not afraid, having been to the mountaintop and having seen the promised land. With this remark he compares himself to the biblical figure Moses, who was able to see the promised land but, on the edge of death, was unable to reach it himself. King proved prophetic: He was assassinated the following day, April 4, 1963, as he stood on the balcony of his Memphis motel.

Thank you very kindly, my friends. As I listened to Ralph Abernathy in his eloquent and generous introduction and then thought about myself, I wondered who he was talking about. It's always good to have your closest friend and associate say something good about you. And Ralph is the best friend that I have in the world.

I'm delighted to see each of you here tonight in spite of a storm warning. You reveal that you are determined to go on anyhow. Something is happening in Memphis, something is happening in our world.

As you know, if I were standing at the beginning of time, with the possibility of general and panoramic view of the whole human history up to now, and the Almighty said to me, "Martin Luther King, which age would you like to live in?"— I would take my mental flight by Egypt through, or rather across the Red Sea, through the wilderness on toward the promised land. And in spite of its magnificence, I wouldn't stop there. I would move on by Greece, and take my mind to Mount Olympus. And I would see Plato, Aristotle, Socrates, Euripides and Aristophanes assembled around the Parthenon as they discussed the great and eternal issues of reality.

But I wouldn't stop there. I would go on, even to the great heyday of the Roman Empire. And I would see developments around there, through various emperors and leaders. But I wouldn't stop there. I would even come up to the day of the Renaissance, and get a quick picture of all that the Renaissance did for the cultural and esthetic life of man. But I wouldn't stop there. I would even go by the way that the man for whom I'm named had his habitat. And I would watch Martin Luther as he tacked his ninety-five theses on the door at the church in Wittenberg.

But I wouldn't stop there. I would come on up even to 1863, and watch a vacillating president by the name of Abraham Lincoln finally come to the conclusion that he had to sign the Emancipation Proclamation. But I wouldn't stop there, I would even come up to the early thirties, and see a man grappling with the problems of the bankruptcy of his nation. And come with an eloquent cry that we have nothing to fear but fear itself.

THE BEST TIME TO LIVE

But I wouldn't stop there. Strangely enough, I would turn to the Almighty, and say, "If you allow me to live just a few years in the second half of the twentieth century, I will be happy." Now that's a strange statement to make, because the world is all messed up. The nation is sick. Trouble is in the land. Confusion all around. That's a strange statement. But I know, somehow, that only when it is dark enough, can you see the stars. And I see God working in this period of the twentieth century in a way that men, in some strange way, are responding—something is happening in our world. The masses of people are rising up. And wherever they are assembled today, whether they are in Johannesburg, South Africa; Nairobi, Kenya; Accra, Ghana; New York City; Atlanta, Georgia; Jackson, Mississippi; or Memphis, Tennessee—the cry is always the same—"We want to be free."

And another reason that I'm happy to live in this period is that we have been forced to a point where we're going to have to grapple with the problems that men have been trying to grapple with through history, but the demands didn't force them to do it. Survival demands that we grapple with them. Men, for years now, have been talking about war and peace. But now, no longer can they just talk about it. It is no longer a choice between violence and nonviolence in this world; it's nonviolence or nonexistence.

THE HUMAN RIGHTS REVOLUTION

That is where we are today. And also in the human rights revolution, if something isn't done, and in a hurry, to bring the colored peoples of the world out of their long years of poverty, their long years of hurt and neglect, the whole world is doomed. Now, I'm just happy that God has allowed me to live in this period, to see what is unfolding. And I'm happy that he's allowed me to be in Memphis.

I can remember, I can remember when Negroes were just going around as Ralph has said, so often, scratching where they didn't itch, and laughing when they were not tickled. But that day is all over. We mean business now, and we are determined to gain our rightful place in God's world.

And that's all this whole thing is about. We aren't engaged in any negative protest and in any negative arguments with anybody. We are saying that we are determined to be men. We are determined to be people. We are saying that we are God's children. And that we don't have to live like we are forced to live.

Now, what does all of this mean in this great period of history? It means that we've got to stay together. We've got to stay together and maintain unity. You know, whenever Pharaoh wanted to prolong the period of slavery in Egypt, he had a favorite, favorite formula for doing it. What was that? He kept the slaves fighting among themselves. But whenever the slaves get together, something happens in Pharaoh's court, and he cannot hold the slaves in slavery. When the slaves get together, that's the beginning of getting out of slavery. Now let us maintain unity.

FOCUSING ON INJUSTICE

Secondly, let us keep the issues where they are. The issue is injustice. The issue is the refusal of Memphis to be fair and honest in its dealings with its public servants, who happen to be sanitation workers. Now, we've got to keep attention on that. That's always the problem with a little violence. You know what happened the other day, and the press dealt only with the window-breaking. I read the articles. They very seldom got around to mentioning the fact that one thousand, three hundred sanitation workers were on strike, and that Memphis is not being fair to them, and that Mayor Loeb is in dire need of a doctor. They didn't get around to that.

Now we're going to march again, and we've got to march again, in order to put the issue where it is supposed to be. And force everybody to see that there are thirteen hundred of God's children here suffering, sometimes going hungry, going through dark and dreary nights wondering how this thing is going to come out. That's the issue. And we've got to say to the nation: we know it's coming out. For when people get caught up with that which is right and they are willing to sacrifice for it, there is no stopping point short of victory.

We aren't going to let any mace stop us. We are masters in our nonviolent movement in disarming police forces; they don't know what to do. I've seen them so often. I remember in Birmingham, Alabama, when we were in that majestic struggle there we would move out of the 16th Street Baptist Church day after day; by the hundreds we would move out. And [Police Commissioner] Bull Connor would tell them to send the dogs forth and they did come; but we just went before the dogs singing, "Ain't gonna let nobody turn me round." Bull Connor next would say, "Turn the fire hoses on." And as I said to you the other night, Bull Connor didn't know history. He knew a kind of physics that somehow didn't relate to the transphysics that we knew about. And that was the fact that there was a certain kind of fire that no water could put out. And we went before the fire hoses; we had known water. If we were Baptist or some other denomination, we had been immersed. If we were Methodist, and some others, we had been sprinkled, but we knew water.

How We Won in Birmingham

That couldn't stop us. And we just went on before the dogs and we would look at them; and we'd go on before the water hoses and we would look at it, and we'd just go on singing "Over my head I see freedom in the air." And then we would be thrown in the paddy wagons, and sometimes we were stacked in there like sardines in a can. And they would throw us in, and old Bull would say, "Take them off," and they did; and we would just go in the paddy wagon singing, "We Shall Overcome." And every now and then we'd get in the jail, and we'd see the jailers looking through the windows being moved by our prayers, and being moved by our words and our songs. And there was a power there which Bull Connor couldn't adjust to; and so we ended up transforming Bull into a steer, and we won our struggle in Birmingham.

Now we've got to go on to Memphis just like that. I call upon you to be with us Monday. Now about injunctions: We have an injunction and we're going into court tomorrow morning to fight this illegal, unconstitutional injunction. All we say to America is, "Be true to what you said on paper." If I lived in China or even Russia, or any totalitarian country, maybe I could understand the denial of certain basic First

Amendment privileges, because they hadn't committed themselves to that over there. But somewhere I read of the freedom of assembly. Somewhere I read of the freedom of speech. Somewhere I read of the freedom of the press. Somewhere I read that the greatness of America is the right to protest for right. And so just as I say, we aren't going to let any injunction turn us around. We are going on. . . .

VOTING WITH THE WALLET

Now the other thing we'll have to do is this: Always anchor our external direct action with the power of economic withdrawal. Now, we are poor people, individually, we are poor when you compare us with white society in America. We are poor. Never stop and forget that collectively, that means all of us together, collectively we are richer than all the nations in the world, with the exception of nine. Did you ever think about that? After you leave the United States, Soviet Russia, Great Britain, West Germany, France, and I could name the others, the Negro collectively is richer than most nations of the world. We have an annual income of more than thirty billion dollars a year, which is more than all of the exports of the United States, and more than the national budget of Canada. Did you know that? That's power right there, if we know how to pool it.

We don't have to argue with anybody. We don't have to curse and go around acting bad with our words. We don't need any bricks and bottles, we don't need any Molotov cocktails, we just need to go around to these stores, and to these massive industries in our country, and say, "God sent us by here, to say to you that you're not treating his children right. And we've come by here to ask you to make the first item on your agenda—fair treatment, where God's children are concerned. Now, if you are not prepared to do that, we do have an agenda that we must follow. And our agenda calls for withdrawing economic support from you."

And so, as a result of this, we are asking you tonight, to go out and tell your neighbors not to buy Coca-Cola in Memphis. Go by and tell them not to buy Sealtest milk. Tell them not to buy—what is the other bread?—Wonder Bread. And what is the other bread company, Jesse? Tell them not to buy Hart's bread. As Jesse Jackson has said, up to now, only the garbage men have been feeling pain; now we must kind of redistribute the pain. We are choosing these companies because they haven't been fair in their hiring policies; and we are choosing them because they can begin the process of saying, they are going to support the needs and the rights of these men who are on strike. And then they can move on downtown and tell Mayor Loeb to do what is right.

But not only that, we've got to strengthen black institutions. I call upon you to take your money out of the banks downtown and deposit your money in Tri-State Bank—we want a "bank-in" movement in Memphis. So go by the savings and loan association. I'm not asking you something that we don't do ourselves at SCLC. Judge Hooks and others will tell you that we have an account here in the savings and loan association from the Southern Christian Leadership Conference. We're just telling you to follow what we're doing. Put your money there. You have six or seven black insurance companies in Memphis. Take out your insurance there. We want to have an "insurance-in."

Now these are some practical things we can do. We begin the process of building a greater economic base. And at the same time, we are putting pressure where it really hurts. I ask you to follow through here.

Now, let me say as I move to my conclusion that we've got to give ourselves to this struggle until the end. Nothing would be more tragic than to stop at this point, in Memphis. We've got to see it through. And when we have our march, you need to be there. Be concerned about your brother. You may not be on strike. But either we go up together, or we go down together. . . .

You know, several years ago, I was in New York City autographing the first book that I had written. And while sitting there autographing books, a demented black woman came up. The only question I heard from her was, "Are you Martin Luther King?"

And I was looking down writing, and I said yes. And the

next minute I felt something beating on my chest. Before I knew it I had been stabbed by this demented woman. I was rushed to Harlem Hospital. It was a dark Saturday afternoon. And that blade had gone through, and the X-rays revealed that the tip of the blade was on the edge of my aorta, the main artery. And once that's punctured, you drown in your own blood—that's the end of you.

It came out in the *New York Times* the next morning, that if I had sneezed, I would have died. Well, about four days later, they allowed me, after the operation, after my chest had been opened, and the blade had been taken out, to move around in the wheel chair in the hospital. They allowed me to read some of the mail that came in, and from all over the states, and the world, kind letters came in. I read a few, but one of them I will never forget. I had received one from the President and the Vice-President. I've forgotten what those telegrams said. I'd received a visit and a letter from the Governor of New York, but I've forgotten what the letter said. But there was another letter that came from a little girl, a young girl who was a student at the White Plains High School. And I looked at that letter, and I'll never forget it. It said simply, "Dear Dr. King: I am a ninth-grade student at the White Plains High School." She said, "While it should not matter, I would like to mention that I am a white girl. I read in the paper of your misfortune, and of your suffering. And I read that if you had sneezed, you would have died. And I'm simply writing you to say that I'm so happy that you didn't sneeze."

WHAT WOULD HAVE BEEN MISSED

And I want to say tonight, I want to say that I am happy that I didn't sneeze. Because if I had sneezed, I wouldn't have been around here in 1960, when students all over the South started sitting-in at lunch counters. And I knew that as they were sitting in, they were really standing up for the best in the American dream. And taking the whole nation back to those great wells of democracy which were dug deep by the Founding Fathers in the Declaration of Independence and the Constitution. If I had sneezed, I wouldn't have been around in 1962, when Negroes in Albany, Georgia, decided to straighten their backs up. And whenever men and women straighten their backs up, they are going somewhere, because a man can't ride your back unless it is bent. If I had sneezed, I wouldn't have been here in 1963, when the black people of Birmingham, Alabama, aroused the conscience of this nation, and brought into being the Civil Rights Bill. If I had sneezed, I wouldn't have had a chance later that year, in August, to try to tell America about a dream that I had had. If I had sneezed, I wouldn't have been down in Selma, Alabama, to see the great movement there. If I had sneezed, I wouldn't have been in Memphis to see the community rally around those brothers and sisters who are suffering. I'm so happy that I didn't sneeze.

And they were telling me, now it doesn't matter now. It really doesn't matter what happens now. I left Atlanta this morning, and as we got started on the plane, there were six of us, the pilot said over the public address system, "We are sorry for the delay, but we have Dr. Martin Luther King on the plane. And to be sure that all of the bags were checked, and to be sure that nothing would be wrong with the plane, we had to check out everything carefully. And we've had the plane protected and guarded all night."

And then I got into Memphis. And some began to say the threats, or talk about the threats that were out. What would happen to me from some of our sick white brothers?

Well, I don't know what will happen now. We've got some difficult days ahead. But it doesn't matter with me now. Because I've been to the mountaintop. And I don't mind. Like anybody, I would like to live a long life. Longevity has its place. But I'm not concerned about that now. I just want to do God's will. And He's allowed me to go up to the mountain. And I've looked over. And I've seen the promised land. I may not get there with you. But I want you to know tonight, that we, as a people, will get to the promised land. And I'm happy, tonight. I'm not worried about anything. I'm not fearing any man. Mine eyes have seen the glory of the coming of the Lord.

CHRONOLOGY

1865
The Thirteenth Amendment outlaws slavery.

1866
In February, Frederick Douglass and other black leaders meet with President Andrew Johnson to press for the right to vote. Johnson is unsympathetic, and the meeting ends in controversy. In May, the Ku Klux Klan, an organization formed to intimidate blacks, is founded in Memphis, Tennessee.

1868
The Fourteenth Amendment extends citizenship to blacks and guarantees due process and equal protection under the law to all citizens.

1870
The Fifteenth Amendment gives black men the right to vote.

1875
Congress approves a civil rights act that guarantees equal rights to blacks in public accommodations and in jury duty.

1881
Tennessee segregates railroad cars. It is later followed by Florida (1887); Mississippi (1888); Texas (1889); Louisiana (1890); Alabama, Kentucky, Arkansas, and Georgia (1891); South Carolina (1898); North Carolina (1899); Virginia (1900); Maryland (1904); and Oklahoma (1907).

1882
Forty-nine blacks are known to be lynched.

1883

The Supreme Court declares the Civil Rights Act of 1875 unconstitutional. Fifty-three blacks are lynched.

1884

Fifty-one blacks are lynched. Each year for the next thirty-five years, between 70 and 161 blacks are lynched. After 1909 the number drops again to about 50 a year.

1895

Booker T. Washington's "Atlanta Compromise" says the "Negro Problem" will be solved by a policy of gradualism and accommodation.

1896

In *Plessy v. Ferguson*, the Supreme Court rules that "separate but equal" facilities satisfy Fourteenth Amendment guarantees, thus giving legal sanction to Jim Crow segregation laws.

1901

After an afternoon meeting with President Theodore Roosevelt, Booker T. Washington accepts Roosevelt's informal invitation to stay for dinner, becoming the first black person to dine at the White House with the president. A furor erupts over the implications of Roosevelt's act.

1903

W.E.B. Du Bois publishes *The Souls of Black Folk*, which rejects the gradualism of Booker T. Washington and calls for black agitation.

1909

The National Association for the Advancement of Colored People is founded. Its main goal is legal reform.

1910

The Baltimore city council approves an ordinance designating the boundaries of black and white neighborhoods. Similar ordinances follow in other cities in the South.

1913

The federal government begins government-wide segregation of workplaces, rest rooms, and lunchrooms.

1917

In April, the United States enters World War I; before it ends, 370,000 black Americans serve in the military. In November, the Supreme Court strikes down a Louisville, Kentucky, ordinance mandating segregated neighborhoods.

1918

Blacks begin migrating north in earnest. Between 1910 and 1930 the black population in the South drops by about 1 million while the black population in the North grows by about 1 million.

1919

Between April and October there are twenty-six race riots.

1920

Marcus Garvey's Universal Negro Improvement Association holds its national convention in Harlem, the traditionally black neighborhood in New York City.

1922–1929

A flourishing of black literature, art, and culture is dubbed the Harlem Renaissance.

1936

Jesse Owens wins four gold medals at the Olympics, which take place in Adolf Hitler's Germany. Owens later says, "I wasn't invited to shake hands with Hitler, but I wasn't invited to the White House to shake hands with the President either."

1941

President Franklin D. Roosevelt issues an executive order forbidding discrimination in defense industries.

1944

The United Negro College Fund is founded.

1946

President Harry S. Truman creates the President's Committee on Civil Rights.

1947

Jackie Robinson becomes the first African American to play major league baseball.

1948

President Truman orders desegregation of the armed forces.

1952

For the first time in seventy-one years, there are no lynchings.

1954

In *Brown v. Board of Education of Topeka, Kansas*, the Supreme Court overturns school segregation laws.

1955

In May, the Supreme Court orders southern states to implement desegregation with "all deliberate speed." In December, Rosa Parks refuses to change seats on a bus in Montgomery, Alabama, setting off a boycott of the bus system; it lasts over a year, until the Supreme Court outlaws bus segregation in the city.

1956

In January, the University of Alabama admits Autherine Lucy, a young black woman, after the Supreme Court orders it to do so; Lucy is later expelled after white students riot. In March, one hundred congressmen from the South sign the Southern Manifesto, which urges resistance to federal desegregation orders.

1957

In January, the Southern Christian Leadership Conference is founded, with Martin Luther King Jr. as president. In August, Congress passes the Voting Rights Bill, the first major civil rights legislation in more than seventy-five years. In September, on what was to be Little Rock Central High's first day as a desegregated school, Arkansas National Guardsmen under orders of Governor Orval Faubus prevent nine black students from entering; eventually, after President Eisenhower orders one thousand paratroopers and ten thousand National Guardsmen to Little Rock, the school is desegregated.

1960

In February, sit-ins in Greensboro, North Carolina, initiate a wave of similar protests throughout southern states. In April, the Student Non-Violent Coordinating Committee is founded in Raleigh, North Carolina. In May, President Eisenhower signs the Civil Rights Act, which authorizes the appointment of federal referees to oversee black voter registration in southern counties. In December, the Supreme Court's ruling in *Boynton v. Virginia* outlaws segregation in interstate bus and railroad facilities.

1961

The Freedom Rides, seeking to end discrimination in the interstate bus system, are met with violent protest at many stops in the South.

1962

President John F. Kennedy orders federal marshals to escort to campus James Meredith, the first black student to enroll at the University of Mississippi. A riot breaks out and two students are killed.

1963

During an April march in Birmingham, Alabama, one of the most severely segregated cities in the country, Martin Luther King Jr. and others are arrested and imprisoned. In June, Governor George Wallace stands in the doorway of a University of Alabama building to signal his blocking of the admission of two black students, and President Kennedy orders the Alabama National Guard to clear the way. In August, the March on Washington is the largest civil rights demonstration in U.S. history, and King delivers his famous "I Have a Dream" speech.

1964

In June, James Chaney, a young black activist, and Andrew Goodman and Michael Schwerner, two white activists, are murdered in Mississippi. In July, President Lyndon B. Johnson signs the Civil Rights Act, which bars discrimination in public accommodations and in hiring. In December, King accepts the Nobel Peace Prize.

1965

In February, Malcolm X is assassinated. In March, during a march from Selma to Montgomery, Alabama, state troopers attack the crowd with tear gas and batons; the event comes to be known as Bloody Sunday. In August, the Voting Rights Act passes and the Watts riots leave thirty-four dead, cause $225 million in property damage, and involve more than thirty-five hundred arrests.

1966

In October, Huey P. Newton and Bobby Seale found the Black Panther Party in Oakland, California. In September,

Stokely Carmichael, head of the Student Non-Violent Coordinating Committee, publishes an article in the *New York Review of Books* endorsing and explaining black power.

1967

In February, the Twenty-Fourth Amendment is ratified, forbidding the use of a poll tax in order to prevent voting. Between May and October, over forty race riots erupt around the country. In August, Thurgood Marshall becomes the first black Supreme Court justice.

1968

In April, Martin Luther King Jr. is assassinated in Memphis, Tennessee. Riots break out in every major city in the country except Indianapolis.

1969

In August, President Richard Nixon orders federal agencies to implement affirmative action programs. In October, the Supreme Court rules in *Alexander v. Holmes* that southern school districts are to desegregate "at once."

1973

In May, Thomas Bradley is elected the first black mayor of Los Angeles. In October, Maynard H. Jackson is elected the first black mayor of Atlanta.

1983

In June, Louisiana's state legislature repeals the last racial classification law in the United States—a stipulation that defines the criterion for being black as having $\frac{1}{32}$ Negro blood. In November, President Ronald Reagan signs the bill establishing the third Monday in January as a federal holiday in honor of King.

1988

Jesse Jackson receives 1,218 delegate votes at the Democratic

National Convention. Michael Dukakis wins the nomination with 2,082 votes.

1991

A black Los Angeles resident, Rodney King, is severely beaten by white police officers, pushing concerns about police brutality into the public spotlight.

1992

In April, the four police officers charged in the Rodney King beating are found not guilty by a jury consisting of ten whites, one Hispanic, and one Asian. Within hours, south-central Los Angeles erupts in riots in which 55 people die, 2,383 are injured, and there is $1 billion in property damage. In August, a federal grand jury charges the officers with violating Rodney King's federally protected civil rights. Ultimately, in April 1993, two of the four officers are convicted and sentenced to two and a half years in prison.

1993

In September, Joycelyn Elders becomes the first African American and the first female U.S. surgeon general. In October, Toni Morrison wins the Nobel Prize in literature, the first black American to do so.

1995

The Million Man March is held in Washington, D.C. Black organizers describe the event as a call to black men to take charge in rebuilding their communities and to show more respect for themselves and their families.

1998

President Bill Clinton awards James Farmer the Medal of Freedom for his civil rights leadership during the 1960s.

1999

The National Capital Planning Commission approves a location on the mall in Washington for a monument to King.

FOR FURTHER RESEARCH

Books

Ralph David Abernathy, *And the Walls Came Tumbling Down.* New York: Harper & Row, 1989.

Floyd B. Barbour, ed., *The Black Power Revolt: A Collection of Essays.* Boston: Porter Sargent, 1968.

Daisy Bates, *The Long Shadow of Little Rock.* New York: David McKay, 1962.

Derrick A. Bell, *And We Are Not Saved: The Elusive Quest for Racial Justice.* New York: HarperCollins, 1987.

———, *Faces at the Bottom of the Well: The Permanence of Racism.* New York: BasicBooks, 1992.

Lerone Bennett Jr., *Before the Mayflower: A History of Black America.* 6th ed. New York: Penguin, 1988.

Robert Blauer, *Racial Oppression in America.* New York: Harper & Row, 1972.

Jack Bloom, *Class, Race, and the Civil Rights Movement.* Bloomington: Indiana University Press, 1987.

Taylor Branch, *Parting the Waters: America in the King Years, 1954–1963.* New York: Simon and Schuster, 1988.

Stokely Carmichael and Charles V. Hamilton, *Black Power: The Politics of Liberation in America.* New York: Random House, 1967.

Cathy Cohen, *The Boundaries of Blackness: AIDS and the Breakdown of Black Politics.* Chicago: University of Chicago Press, 1999.

Vicki L. Crawford, Jacqueline Anne Rouse, and Barbara Woods, eds., *Women in the Civil Rights Movement.* Brooklyn, NY: Carlson, 1990.

Angela Y. Davis, *Women, Race, and Class.* New York: Random House, 1981.

W.E.B. Du Bois, *The Souls of Black Folk.* 1903. Reprint, New York: Alfred A. Knopf, 1993.

Charles W. Eagles, ed., *The Civil Rights Movement in America.* Jackson: University Press of Mississippi, 1986.

Ralph Ellison, *Invisible Man.* New York: Vintage Books, 1995.

Frantz Fanon, *Black Skin, White Masks.* Trans. Charles Lam Markmann. New York: Grove, 1967.

James Farmer, *Lay Bare the Heart: An Autobiography of the Civil Rights Movement.* New York: Arbor House, 1985.

Henry Louis Gates Jr. and Cornel West, *The Future of the Race.* New York: Knopf, 1996.

Rhoda L. Goldstein, ed., *Black Life and Culture in the United States.* New York: Thomas Y. Crowell, 1971.

Henry Hampton, Steve Fager, and Sarah Flynn, *Voices of Freedom: An Oral History of the Civil Rights Movement from the 1950s Through the 1980s.* New York: Bantam Books, 1990.

Don Hazen, ed., *Inside the L.A. Riots: What Really Happened and Why It Will Happen Again: Essays and Articles by More than Sixty of America's Leading Independent Writers and Journalists.* New York: Institute for Alternative Journalism, 1992.

bell hooks, *Black Looks: Race and Representation.* Boston: South End, 1992.

Martin Luther King Jr., *I Have a Dream: Writings and Speeches That Changed the World.* Ed. J. Melvin. San Francisco: Harper, 1986.

Gerda Lerner, ed., *Black Women in White America: A Documentary History*. New York: Vintage Books, 1973.

Gunnar Myrdal, *An American Dilemma: The Negro Problem and Modern Democracy*. New York: Harper & Brothers, 1944.

Booker T. Washington, *Up from Slavery*. Toronto: Bantam, 1956.

Robert Weisbort, *Freedom Bound: A History of America's Civil Rights Movement*. New York: W.W. Norton, 1990.

Patricia Williams, *The Alchemy of Race and Rights*. Cambridge, MA: Harvard University Press, 1991.

Malcolm X, *By Any Means Necessary*. 2nd ed. New York: Pathfinder, 1992.

Robert L. Zangrando, *The NAACP Crusade Against Lynching*. Philadelphia: Temple University Press, 1980.

Periodicals

George J. Church, "Cries of Relief," *Time*, April 26, 1993.

John Cloud, "The KGB of Mississippi," *Time*, March 30, 1998.

David Brion Davis, "Free at Last: The Enduring Legacy of the South's Civil War Victory," *New York Times*, August 26, 2001.

William R. Doerner, "We Still Have a Dream: Twenty Years Later, Thousands March in Washington for a Medley of Causes," *Time*, September 5, 1983.

Michael Fletcher, "Putting a Price on Slavery's Legacy; Call for Reparations Builds as Blacks Tally History's Toll," *Washington Post*, December 26, 2000.

Marshall Frady, "The Children of Malcolm," *New Yorker*, May 16, 1994.

Henry Louis Gates Jr., "Whose Canon Is It, Anyway?" *New York Times Book Review*, February 26, 1989.

Paul Good, "A White Look at Black Power," *Nation*, August 8, 1966.

Jonathan Hicks, "Answering the March's Call," *New York Times*, December 29, 1995.

Michael Janofsky, "The March on Washington," *New York Times*, October 16, 1995.

Wendy Kaminer, "Up from Reparations," *American Prospect*, May 22, 2000.

Joe Klein, "The End of Affirmative Action," *Newsweek*, February 13, 1995.

Jacob V. Lamar, "Honoring Justice's Drum Major," *Time*, January 27, 1986.

Tamar Lewin, "Calls for Slavery Restitution Getting Louder," *New York Times*, June 4, 2001.

Tom Morganthau, "The New Frontier for Civil Rights," *Newsweek*, November 29, 1993.

Michael Riley, "Confessions of a Former Segregationist," *Time*, March 2, 1992.

Vern E. Smith, "Debating the Wages of Slavery," *Newsweek*, August 27, 2001.

Mark Starr, "Civil Rights, Reagan Style," *Newsweek*, January 30, 1984.

Paul Starr, "Race and Reparations: A New Road to Healing Black America," *Washington Post*, April 19, 1992.

James Traub, "Separate and Equal," *Atlantic Monthly*, September 1991.

INDEX

school
  in Little Rock, 22
  at University of Alabama, 24–25
  at University of Mississippi,
    63–64, 192–96
  white resistance to, 59–60, 61–63
  token, in the North, 86
Diallo, Amadou, 160
Dorrough, Charles, 80
Douglass, Frederick, 32
Drew, Charles, 20
Dubinsky, David, 88
Du Bois, W.E.B., 17, 40
Duckett, Alfred, 112
Dukakis, Mike, 148

education
  quality of, for blacks, 128–29
  see also desegregation, school
Education and Attitude Change
  (Stember), 85
Eisenhower, Dwight D., 21, 85
Elders, Joycelyn, 150
Ellison, Ralph, 76
Emancipation Proclamation, 12
employment discrimination
  institutional, 136
  prohibition of, 134–35
  see also affirmative action
Enforcement Acts, 14
Espy, Mike, 150
Evers, Medgar, 25, 189
Executive Order 11246, 134, 137

Fair Employment Opportunity
  Commission, 142
Fair Employment Practices
  Commission, 20
Farrad, Wadi, 101
Faubus, Orville, 22
Federal Bureau of Investigation
  Black Panther Party and, 104
  surveillance of Martin Luther King
    Jr. by, 123
Ferguson, John, 16
Fifteenth Amendment, 14
Foreman, James, 174

Fourteenth Amendment, 14
Franklin, John Hope, 149, 181
Freedom Rides (1961), 23–24, 76
  white disapproval of, 90
Friedman, Bernard A., 169
Friedman, Murray, 84
From Slavery to Freedom (Franklin),
  181
Fugitive Slave Act, 12–13
Fullinwider, Robert K., 134

Gallup Poll
  on approval of Freedom Rides, 90
  on white attitudes toward
    desegregation, 85
Gandhi, Mohandas K., 19, 71
Garrison, William Lloyd, 17
Garrow, David J., 124
Garvey, Marcus, 18–19, 95
Gassama, Ibrahim, 175
Gibson, James, 124
Gilder, George, 146
Ginsburg, Ruth Bader, 171
Goodman, Andrew, 26
Gore, Al, 150
Great Society
  cutbacks in, 98
Green, Andre, 125
Griggs v. Duke Power Company, 135

Hamer, Fannie Lou, 99
Hampton, Fred, 104
Hardy, John, 81
Harlan, John Marshall, 16
Harlem Renaissance, 18–19
Harlins, Latasha, 155–56
Hentoff, Nat, 127
Herrnstein, Richard, 151
Hispanics
  conflicts between blacks and,
    154–56
Holliday, George, 156
Hoover, J. Edgar, 123
Hopwood v. Texas, 165, 169, 170, 172
Horton, James Oliver, 144
Horton, Lois E., 144
Horton, Willie, 148